BRAVE NEW WAR

THE NEXT STAGE OF TERRORISM AND THE END OF GLOBALIZATION

John Robb

John Wiley & Sons, Inc.

Published by John Wiley & Sons, Inc., Hoboken, New Jersey
Published simultaneously in Canada

Wiley Bicentennial Logo: Richard J. Pacifico

For general information about our other products and services, please contact our Customer Care Department within the United States at (800) 762-2974, outside the United States at (317) 572-3993 or fax (317) 572-4002.

Wiley also publishes its books in a variety of electronic formats. Some content that appears in print may not be available in electronic books. For more information about Wiley products, visit our web site at www.wiley.com.

Library of Congress Cataloging-in-Publication Data:

Robb, John, date.
    Brave new war: the next stage of terrorism and the end of
globalization / John Robb.
        p. cm.
    Includes bibliographical references and index.
    ISBN 978-0-471-78079-3
    1. Terrorism. 2. Guerrilla warfare. 3. Transnational crime.
4. Security, International. 5. National security. 6. Private security
services. 7. Globalization. I. Title.
    HV6431.R625 2007
    363.325—dc22

                                                2006029354

Printed in the United States of America

10 9 8 7 6 5 4 3 2

CONTENTS

Foreword by James Fallows   v
Preface   xiii

Part I
THE FUTURE OF WAR IS NOW

1 The Superempowered Competition   3
2 Disorder on the Doorstep   12
3 A New Strategic Weapon   33

Part II
GLOBAL GUERRILLAS

4 The Long Tail of Warfare Emerges   67
5 Systems Disruption   94
6 Open-Source Warfare   111

Part III
HOW GLOBALIZATION WILL PUT
AN END TO GLOBALIZATION

7 Guerrilla Entrepreneurs   133
8 Rethinking Security   152
9 A Brittle Security Breakdown   184

Notes	189
Further Reading	194
Index	196

FOREWORD
by James Fallows

Through the spring and summer of 2006, I talked with a wide variety of experts about the current state of the conflict that Osama bin Laden thinks of as the world jihad and that the U.S. government has called the "global war on terror" and the "long war." About half of the authorities I spoke with were from military or intelligence organizations; the others were academics or members of think tanks, plus a few businesspeople. I sought their views for an article I was writing for the *Atlantic Monthly*. Among the most memorable of these interviews was a man I had met briefly once before: John Robb.

From the interviewees as a whole, I was surprised by one implicitly optimistic theme. This did not have to do with the war in Iraq, which many of them had originally supported but which nearly all had come to see as an unbounded disaster for the United States. Nor was it necessarily based on a belief that the United States would figure out the shrewdest way to protect its people, interests, and institutions from terrorist-style disruptions that were sure to be a feature of twenty-first-century life.

Instead it had to do with America's success up to that point in disrupting Osama bin Laden's own "al-Qaeda Central" organization—and America's *potential* ability to recast the larger global "war of ideas" in a way far more likely to win support or sympathy and diminish sources of hostility around the world. This, after all, had been a crucial element of the West policy throughout the Cold War—hardly the only element, given the battles and wars the United States fought and the CIA projects and dictators it funded as part of the larger struggle against the Soviet Union. As Sir Richard Dearlove, the former director of Britain's secret intelligence agency, MI-6, and one of the people I interviewed, put it, by the end of the Cold War there was no doubt about which side stood on the moral high ground. "Potential recruits would come to us because they believed in the cause," he said. "This made our work much easier." Dearlove and countless others argued that the United States had gravely weakened its position by seeming to ignore its long-standing constitutional principles, in internal checks-and-balances and in its practices around the world. "America's cause is doomed unless it regains the moral high ground," Dearlove said. But, as he and many others suggested, this should be a correctable situation, given the resilience of many western societies and the fundamental appeal of the modern model of tolerant civil society.

The implicit optimism of this outlook was surprising because it was a contrast to most public discourse since the al-Qaeda attacks of 2001. The crudest version of the pessimist message was the endless governmental warnings that the "evil doers" were ceaselessly planning to attack again, because they "hate our freedom." Whether officials in the Bush administration actually thought the motivation was that simple is hard to tell. All I know, from reporting, is that virtually no one with first-hand operating experience in fighting or analyzing terrorist movements agrees. (Resentment of the western world's affluence and perceived licentiousness is no doubt part of al-Qaeda's impulse, but it's hardly the main part. As no less an authority than Osama bin Laden put it in a tape released just before the 2004 election, if al-Qaeda was so opposed to liberties, "Why did we not attack Sweden?" Political grievances against western, especially U.S., policies have always come at the top of al-Qaeda's list of complaints.)

The more sophisticated pessimistic argument had to do with the inherent vulnerability of big, open societies. By this reasoning, the United States was locked into an asymmetric struggle in which many advantages lay on the other side. Any of the tens of millions of foreigners entering the country each year could, in theory, be an enemy operative—to say nothing of the millions of potential recruits already in place. Any of the dozens of ports, the scores of natural-gas plants and nuclear facilities, the hundreds of important bridges and tunnels, or the thousands of shopping malls, office towers, or sporting facilities could be the next target of attack. It is impossible to protect them all, and even trying could ruin America's social fabric and public finances. The worst part of the "asymmetric" predicament is the helplessness, as America's officials and its public wait for an attack they know they cannot prevent.

Then we come to John Robb. His analysis is in many ways darker even than the conventionally pessimistic view—though if properly understood it contains practical and positive elements as well. But mainly it is far more sophisticated than just about anything else the public is used to hearing about the nature of the challenge it faces. This book is not a complete answer to America's problems in defending itself while preserving its liberties. No book is, or could be. But it is a very serious and valuable contribution.

When I spoke with Robb in 2006, he pointed out how easy it is for terrorists to disrupt society's normal operations—think of daily life in Israel, or England under assault from the IRA. But large-scale symbolic shock, of the type so stunningly achieved on September 11 and advocated by bin Laden ever since, is difficult to repeat or sustain. "There are diminishing returns on symbolic terrorism," he told me then. "Each time it happens, the public becomes desensitized, and the media pays less attention." To maintain the level of terror, each attack must top the previous one, and in Robb's view, "Nothing will ever top 9/11." He allows for the obvious and significant exception of terrorists getting hold of a nuclear weapon. But, like most people I interviewed, he says this is harder and less likely than the public assumes. Moreover, if nuclear weapons constitute the one true existential threat, then countering the proliferation of those weapons themselves is what American policy should address, more than fighting terrorism in general. For a big, coordinated, nonnuclear attack, he says, "the number of people involved is substantial, the lead time is long, the degree of coordination is great, and the specific skills you need are considerable. It's not realistic for al-Qaeda anymore."

But he went on to argue, convincingly and disturbingly, that the rise of small-scale, "do-it-yourself" terrorism could in many ways be more troublesome than the big, centrally planned attacks the United States seemed to be most concerned about. And this led naturally to the most original part of his argument, and the one developed fully in this book: how the modern environment of networks and complex human systems required a completely different understanding of terms like *defense*, *offense*, *aggression*, and *security*. Many people argue that blunting al-Qaeda's ability to launch huge, spectacular attacks will protect developed societies in a significant way. Anyone who reads this book will recognize why a shift to more dispersed, localized, smaller-scale threats could, in the long run, prove even more threatening.

Already there are illustrations of the phenomena Robb warns about in his book (and which he chronicles day by day on his Global Guerrillas Web site). They all involve the idea of turning the complexity and power of a developed modern economy from strengths to vulnerabilities. For instance, documents captured after 9/11 showed that bin Laden hoped to provoke the United States into an invasion and occupation that would drain the United States financially, estrange it from its allies diplomatically, and turn the Islamic world against it culturally and emotionally. His only error was to think that the place where Americans would think this would happen would be Afghanistan rather than Iraq.

Many al-Qaeda documents refer to the importance of sapping American economic strength as a step toward reducing America's ability to throw its weight around in the Middle East. Bin Laden imagined this would happen largely through attacks on America's oil supply. This is still a goal. For instance, a 2004 fatwa from the imprisoned head of al-Qaeda in Saudi Arabia declared that targeting oil pipelines and refineries was a legitimate form of economic jihad—and that economic jihad "is one of the most powerful ways in which we can take revenge on the infidels during this present stage." The fatwa went on to offer an analysis many economists would be proud of, laying out all the steps that would lead from a less-secure oil supply to a less-productive American economy and ultimately to a run on the dollar. (It also emphasized that oil wells themselves should be attacked only as a last resort, because news coverage of the smoke and fires would hurt al-Qaeda's image.)

Another form of self-inflicted damage has hurt the United States even more than bin Laden appears to have foreseen. This is the systematic drag on public and private resources created by the undifferentiated need to be "secure." The effect is most obvious on the public level. "The economy as a whole took six months or so to recover from the effects of 9/11," Richard Clarke told me during the same set of interviews in 2006. "The federal budget never recovered. The federal budget is in a permanent mess, to a large degree because of 9/11." A total of five people died from anthrax spores sent through the mail shortly after 9/11. In his book *Overblown*, John Mueller of Ohio State points out that the U.S. Postal Service will eventually spend about $5 billion on protective screening equipment and other measures in response to the anthrax threat, or about $1 billion per fatality. Each new security guard, each extra checkpoint or biometric measure, is both a direct cost and an indirect drag on economic flexibility. If bin Laden hadn't fully anticipated this effect, he certainly recognized it after it occurred. In his statement just before the 2004 election, he quoted the finding of the Royal Institute of International Affairs to the effect that the total cost, direct and indirect, to the United States of the 9/11 attacks was at least $500 billion. Bin Laden gleefully pointed out that the attacks had cost al-Qaeda about $500,000, for a million-to-one payoff ratio. America's deficit spending for Iraq and homeland security was, he said, "evidence of the success of the bleed-until-bankruptcy plan, with Allah's permission."

Early in 2004, a Saudi exile named Saad al-Faqih was interviewed by the online publication *Terrorism Monitor*. Al-Faqih, who leads an opposition group seeking political reform in Saudi Arabia, is a longtime observer of his fellow Saudi Osama bin Laden and of the evolution of bin Laden's doctrine for al-Qaeda. In the interview, al-Faqih said that for nearly a decade, bin Laden and al-Zawahiri had followed a powerful grand strategy for confronting the United States. Their approach boiled down to "superpower baiting"—the term John Robb used when I asked him about it in 2006. The most predictable thing about Americans, in this view—and therefore another of their vulnerabilities—was that they would rise to the bait of a challenge or provocation.

The United States is immeasurably stronger than al-Qaeda, but against jujitsu forms of attack its strength has been its disadvantage. The predictability of the U.S. response has allowed opponents to turn our bulk and momentum against us. Al-Qaeda can do more harm to the United States than to, say, Italy, because the self-damaging potential of an uncontrolled American reaction is so vast.

How can the United States escape this trap? This book does not provide anything so crisp as a one-sentence answer, but it does suggest the right framework with which to approach the question. One step Robb suggested to me was entirely rethinking the notion of a "war" against a stateless, dispersed enemy. "De-escalation of the rhetoric is the first step," Robb told me. "It is hard for insurgents to handle de-escalation." War encourages a simple classification of the world into ally or enemy. This polarization gives dispersed terrorist groups a unity they might not have on their own. Rather than dividing its enemies, the United States has inadvertently united them.

There are many more steps—of mindset, even more than of action—that will be evident to readers by the time they finish this book. I don't agree with every one of the perspectives and recommendations offered here, and I expect many readers will find areas where they differ from Robb. But I am very glad to have read this book, and I expect others will be, too.

Shanghai, China
February 2007

PREFACE

As I was working on this book in early 2006, in my self-imposed exile in a Florida vacation home (without the distraction of Internet access), I received some interesting news through an unusual source: the TV. (Does anyone really get news from that device anymore?) In less than forty-eight hours, there were two attacks by al-Qaeda that nearly sank U.S. policy in the Middle East.

The first attack, made against the Samarra mosque in Iraq, so neatly tore at the social fabric of the country that it nearly plunged that nation into an immediate and full-blown civil war. A small gang of guerrillas successfully destroyed the gilded dome of the Al-Askari mosque, one of the holiest sites in Shia Islam. The country quickly erupted in protests as tens of thousands of Shiite Muslims took to the streets. While an immediate collapse into civil war was averted, it is now still in play but growing at a slower, organic rate.

Not satisfied with that instability, two days later al-Qaeda also attempted an attack in Saudi Arabia on a critical oil facility in Abqaiq that processes oil from the world's biggest oil field in Ghawar. Saudi security forces opened fire on two cars packed with explosives, preventing them from reaching their target. This attack almost cut global

oil production, in a very tight market, by millions of barrels a day. If it had succeeded, we would be paying over
$100 a barrel for oil right now.

Quickly planned, and executed with only limited personnel and resources, both of these events were nearly utter
catastrophes. Despite that, both caught much of the world
by surprise. If we're unable to predict and prevent these
types of out-of-the-blue events, after nearly five years of
fighting terrorism, then whatever we are doing is clearly
not working.

This book is about rapid, chaotic, and unexpected
events, such as those that we witnessed over that fateful
forty-eight hours. I call events like these black swans—
events so different from what we know, so unpredictable
and hidden by uncertainty, that they are impossible to predict with accuracy. While we're busy working to protect
ourselves against the previous attack, we can expect more
black swans, because they are being manufactured by our
foes at an increasing frequency.

The reasons for this are twofold. The first is that we
now live in an extremely complex global system. It is too
complex for any single state, or group of states, to keep
under control. As a result, most of the systems we have
built over the last several centuries to dampen the excesses
of instability—enabled by markets, travel, communication, and other global systems—are now ineffectual.

The second reason is that certain people—guerrillas—
are now intentionally introducing instability into these global systems by attacking critical systems, both social and
economic. These manufactured instabilities are almost
impossible to control. Additionally, many of the things we
have tried in order to stop these negative actors have only
made matters worse, not better.

With this book, I hope I have something to add to the thinking about this topic. My experience may help. I am naturally a "red team" player—a person who thinks like the opposition. This experience began in the military, where I worked with Delta and Seal Team 6 chasing terrorists around the world. I was trained to be a smuggler, a person who could cross international boundaries like a ghost. My second major career path was as another type of outsider: an entrepreneur. On numerous occasions, I spotted trends in the fast-moving technology industry, which allowed me to build companies that push aside traditional companies and seize fresh opportunities.

Because of this combination of experience and mindset, I often find my take on what's in the news every day to be radically different from the common wisdom. I keep coming back to the way terrorism and guerrilla warfare is rapidly evolving to allow nonstate networks to challenge the structure and order of nation-states. It is a change on par with the rise of the Internet and China, and will dramatically change how you and your children view security.

By the time the open-source, systems-disrupting, transnational crime–fueled sons of global fragmentation come to dominate the front of your morning newspaper, it may be too late to make an easy transition. Many of our global suppliers of critical resources will be severely disrupted, the global economy will be under extreme levels of stress, and our view of the federal government's role in security will be unalterably changed. I don't think anything that will happen will ultimately destroy us (I'm at the core an optimist), but the transition period will certainly be much more difficult than it has to be if we don't prepare.

War in the twenty-first century will be very different from what we've come to expect. I've done my best to point out the signs of this new model's emerging threats, provide copious analysis on its origins, construct a model of the way it works, and generate some insight into how its maturation will affect our lives. I've even offered some ideas on how we can survive this (although I doubt anybody will pay attention to them since they don't provide the level of pork barrel spending current arrangements do). Lastly, it should be fast paced enough to hold your attention.

Before you read on, I have three requests:

1. Please don't consider this book to be another "terrorist book," because it isn't. I'll leave that to the professional fearmongers of the counterterrorism and political communities.
2. Please enjoy this book (to the extent you can), and fasten your seat belts. It should be a good ride.
3. This book has lots of ideas (almost too many). Please treat it as a buffet table and not a five-course meal. Take what you want of my vision of the future and discard the rest with alacrity.

Part I

THE FUTURE OF WAR IS NOW

1

THE SUPEREMPOWERED COMPETITION

The near future holds mind-bending promise for American business.[1] Globalization is prying open vast new markets. Technology is plowing ahead, fueling—and transforming—entire industries, creating services we never thought possible. Clever people worldwide are capitalizing every which way. But because globalization and technology are morally neutral forces, they can also drive change of a different sort. We saw this very clearly on September 11, 2001, and are seeing it now in Iraq and in conflicts around the world. In short, despite the aura of limitless possibility, our lives are evolving in ways we can control only if we recognize the new landscape. It's time to take an unblinking look.

We have entered the age of the faceless, agile enemy. From London to Madrid to Nigeria to Russia, stateless terrorist groups have emerged to score blow after blow against us. Driven by cultural fragmentation, schooled in the most sophisticated technologies, and fueled by transnational crime, these groups are forcing corporations and individuals to develop new ways of defending themselves.

The end result of this struggle will be a new, more resilient approach to national security, one built not around the state but around private citizens and companies. That new system will change how we live and work—for the better, in many ways—but the road getting there may seem long at times.

The conflict in Iraq has foreshadowed the future of global security in much the same way that the Spanish civil war prefigured World War II: it's become a testing ground, a dry run for something much larger. Unlike previous insurgencies, the one in Iraq comprises seventy-five to one hundred small, diverse, and autonomous groups of zealots, patriots, and criminals alike. These groups, of course, have access to many of the same tools we do—from satellite phones to engineering degrees—and they use them every bit as effectively. But their single most important asset is their organizational structure, an open-source community network—one that seems to me quite similar to what we see in the software industry. That's how they're able to continually stay one step ahead of us. It is an extremely innovative structure, sadly, and it results in decision-making cycles much shorter than those of the U.S. military. Indeed, because the insurgents in Iraq lack a recognizable center of gravity—a leadership structure or an ideology—they are nearly immune to the application of conventional military force. Like Microsoft, the software superpower, the United States hasn't found its match in a Goliath competitor similar to itself, but in a loose, self-tuning network.

In Iraq, we've also witnessed the convergence of international crime and terrorism as they provide ample fuel and a global platform for these new enemies. Al-Qaeda's attack on Madrid, for example, was funded by the sale of the drug ecstasy. Moisés Naim, a former Venezuelan minister of trade and industry and the editor and publisher of the magazine *Foreign Policy,* documented this trend in his insightful book *Illicit: How Smugglers, Traffickers, and Copycats Are Hijacking the Global Economy.* Globalization has fostered the development of a huge criminal economy that boasts a technologically leveraged global supply chain (like Wal-Mart's) and can handle everything from human trafficking (eastern Europe) to illicit drugs (Asia and South America), pirated goods (Southeast Asia), arms (Central Asia), and money laundering (everywhere). Naim puts the value of that economy at between $2 and $3 trillion a year. He says it is expanding at *seven times* the rate of legitimate world trade.

This terrorist-criminal symbiosis becomes even more powerful when considered next to the most disturbing sign coming out of Iraq: the terrorists have developed the ability to fight nation-states strategically—without weapons of mass destruction. This new method is called *systems disruption,* a simple way of attacking the critical networks (electricity, oil, gas, water, communications, and transportation) that underpin modern life. Such disruptions are designed to erode the target state's legitimacy, to drive it to failure by keeping it from providing the services it must deliver in order to command the allegiance of its citizens. Over the past two years, attacks on the oil and electricity networks in Iraq have reduced and held delivery of these critical services below prewar levels, with a disastrous effect on the country, its people, and its economy.

The early examples of systems disruption in Iraq and elsewhere are ominous. If these techniques are even lightly applied to the fragile electrical and oil-gas systems in Russia, Saudi Arabia, or anywhere in the target-rich West, we could see a rapid onset of economic and political chaos unmatched since the advent of the blitzkrieg. (India's January arrest of militants with explosives in Hyderabad suggests that the country's high-tech industry could be a new target.) It's even worse when we consider the asymmetry of the economics involved: one small attack on an oil pipeline in southeast Iraq, conducted for an estimated $2,000, cost the Iraqi government more than $500 million in lost oil revenues. That is a return on investment of 25 million percent.

Now that the tipping point has been reached, the rise of global virtual states—with their thriving criminal economies, innovative networks, and hyperefficient war craft—will rapidly undermine public confidence in our national-security systems. In fact, this process has already begun. We've seen disruption of our oil supply in Iraq, Nigeria, Venezuela, and Colombia; the market's fear of more disruptions contributes mightily to the current high prices for oil. As these disruptions continue, the damage will spill over into the very structure of our society. Our profligate U.S. Department of Defense, reeling from its inability to defend our borders on 9/11 or to pacify even a small country like Iraq, will increasingly be seen as obsolete.

TECHNOLOGICAL MULTIPLIERS

Accustomed to living with almost routine scientific breakthroughs, we have yet to come to terms with the fact that the most compelling 21st-century technologies—robotics, genetic engineering, and nanotechnology—pose a different threat than the technologies that have come before. Specifically, robots, engineered organisms, and nanobots share a dangerous amplifying factor: They can self-replicate. A bomb is blown up only once—but one bot can become many, and quickly get out of control.

—Bill Joy, cofounder and chief scientist of Sun Microsystems[2]

From a security perspective, the most disturbing aspect of 9/11 wasn't the horrible destruction, but that the men who attacked us on that day didn't even factor the opposition of the U.S. military into their planning. Despite tens of trillions of dollars spent on defense over the last decades, this military force proved ineffectual as a deterrent at the point when we needed it most.

Worse yet, nothing has changed since then. The U.S. military, in budget after budget since 9/11, has continued to plan, build, and fund forces dedicated to fighting a great power war—with an increasing emphasis on China and to a lesser extent Iran. Even the guerrilla war in Iraq hasn't forced any substantive changes to our defense structure. This isn't due to a nefarious plot at the highest levels of government. It is due to the fundamental inability of the nation-state to conceptualize a role that makes sense in fighting and deterring the emerging threat.

The real threat, as seen in the rapid rise in global terrorism over the past five years, is that this threat isn't another state but rather the superempowered group. This group, riding on the leverage provided by rapid technology improvement and global integration, is and will remain the major threat to our way of life.

To really understand this future, you need to discard the idea of state-versus-state conflict. That age is over. It ended with the rise of nuclear weapons, the integration of the world's economies, and the end of the cold war. Wars between states are now, for all intents and purposes, obsolete. The real remaining threat posed by wars between states, in those rare cases when they do occur by choice, is that they will create a vacuum within which these non-state groups can thrive. Every time we shuffle the playing cards with state-versus-state conflict, we will find that we are ultimately less well off than before it occurred.

Given the withering away of state-versus-state conflict, we shouldn't assume that the reasons for warfare have departed with it. All the economic, environmental, social, religious, and ethnic drivers of conflict are still in place. In fact, there is every reason to believe they actually may be strengthening, given the fragmenting power of the Internet. The real change is that wars fought over these issues won't be fought by states, but at a level below that of the state.

This new granular level, the realm of superempowered groups, is where the seeds of epochal conflict now reside. Unfortunately, as demonstrated by 9/11 and Iraq, these groups have now gained the ability to wage war on states and win. How this came about should sound familiar. It leverages the tools you use every day.

The rise of superempowered groups is part of a larger historical trend. This trend is in the process of putting ever-more-powerful technological tools and the knowledge of how to use them into an ever-increasing number of hands. Economically, this is fantastic news. This transfer of technological leverage means faster productivity growth and improvements in incomes. Within the context of war, however, this is dire news, because this trend dictates that technology will leverage the ability of individuals and small groups to wage war with equal alacrity.

Within this larger context, the conflict we are currently engaged in is merely a waypoint on this trend line. The threshold necessary for small groups to conduct warfare has finally been breached, and we are only starting to feel its effects. Over time, perhaps in as little as twenty years, and as the leverage provided by technology increases, this threshold will finally reach its culmination—*with the ability of one man to declare war on the world and win.* Now, with every improvement in genetic engineering and nanotechnology (only some of many potential threats), we come closer to the day when a single individual will have the budget, the knowledge, and the tools necessary to make this future possible.

Years ago, I had a college physics instructor who was on leave from his primary job: designing nuclear weapons for the military. He was, and likely still is, a tightly controlled person. The knowledge he held in his head was dangerous, and as a result the government carefully controlled his movements. Those days of tight control are quickly ending, however. The knowledge of dangerous technologies that was typically harnessed and closely monitored by the government is quickly proliferating beyond its control. This knowledge is now becoming something a great many people will possess and be able to use. Furthermore, this knowledge is now global, driven by the winds of ever-increasing interconnectivity.

The root of this transformation is the accelerating rate of change in the power of ubiquitously available technology. Over the last twenty years or so, the ability to manipulate and use technology has decentralized to become widely accessible. Not only are the tools accelerating in power but also the breadth of access to these tools has become nearly universal.

Technology's Paradox

It's well known that technology can be used for both good and bad ends. The classic example of this is nuclear power (although many would argue that it is entirely bad). Under the classic rules of this paradox, these rogue technologies occurred only rarely and required a nation-state to produce them.

Today's rules are different. Technology is now rapidly advancing across a broad front, and the barriers to usage have dropped to nothing. A recent example of this new rule set is Japan's realization that Sony's PlayStation 2 console has sufficient graphics-crunching capability to pilot a missile to its desired target.[3] In essence, anyone can now buy a critical component for an advanced weapons guidance system on eBay for $200.

The reason for this breakout from technology's historically glacial and seemingly linear pace of improvement is Moore's law. Named for a claim made by Gordon E. Moore, the cofounder of Intel in the 1960s, Moore's law states that the number of transistors on a computer chip (integrated circuit) doubles every eighteen months.

Moore was right, and this exponential pace of improvement has been holding steady within this technology cycle since the middle of the twentieth century. In fact, the technologist Ray Kurzweil has shown that it reaches back to technology cycles before the integrated circuit as well. It is only now making its effects known, as the curve of this exponential rate of improvement breaks above the horizon of linear progress.

Furthermore, since this improvement was packaged in a product that is globally accessible (the computer chip), Moore's law has now begun to permeate every field of technology. For the purposes of our discussion, the fact that Moore's law is packaged in an affordable form means that the tools available to individuals are also improving at an exponential pace. You can now run programs on your laptop that previously would have taken a team of accountants, a laboratory of biologists, a pool of secretaries, or a group of engineers to accomplish.

Right behind Moore's law is a second inexorable trend. That trend is the increasing power and complexity provided by a ubiquitous global network. That network, of course, is the Internet, and its most important application, the World Wide Web, is an example of the reverse of the dual use of technology since the Internet started within the Department of Defense. Again, within economic terms this is a cornucopia of plenty, powering a bewildering, complex array of global goods and services. Within the context of warfare, however, it takes a different form altogether.

The leverage provided by these technologies has finally reached a point where small superempowered groups, and not yet individuals, now have the capability to challenge the state in warfare and win. For the most part, these non-state groups have been using these new technologies mostly as a means to recruit, train, equip, and mobilize decentralized organizations. A more ominous trend has developed, however. These groups are quickly learning to use—against us—the technologies we use daily.

Airplanes are being turned into flying bombs, cell phone networks are being used to simultaneously detonate bombs from miles away, and critical computer networks are being hacked. More important, a growing number of attacks are being made on the underlying computerized networks that support our very economic fabric: from the oil distribution system to electricity grids. If this is what we are already seeing with the first iteration of this trend, then it is a safe bet that the capability to instantly leverage the rapid technological progress under way will soon be dangerous enough to threaten the world with catastrophe.

It's my belief that our response to the threats posed by the superempowered groups that we face today will define our survivability against the threat of extermination in the future. If we continue to expect the next major terrorist attack to look just like the last one, the odds will not be in our favor.

2

DISORDER ON THE DOORSTEP

The explosives were easy to set. The location they chose was safe, far from the motley collection of Iraqi forces and private contractors dedicated to the protection of Iraq's oil infrastructure. Their maps were highly accurate and showed exactly which pipeline, buried in a maze of others, was the critical one they wanted. They had only to dig a six-foot hole in the sandy soil, place the charges, and hit the ignition switch. The explosion itself wasn't even that large, but it was more than sufficient to burst the shell of the forty-eight-inch high-pressure oil line. Immediately, a flood of oil poured from the rupture, forming a small pool. Twenty-four hours later, with over 370,000 barrels of oil a day to draw from in the pipe, the pool had grown into a vast black lake overlaid with fetid fumes.

The repair crews, guarded by mercenary Ghurkas, stumbled to the scene along washed-out roads. In the 120-degree heat of the Iraqi summer, work went at a snail's pace, and because of security concerns nighttime work was ruled out. As the oil was drained away, Halliburton engineers paced nervously at the lake's edge, enforcing a hotly contested smoking ban on Iraqi repair crews. Nearly a week later, the repairs were complete, despite a dark comedy of errors, shortages, and missteps.

The financial impact of this sabotage was massive. The struggling Iraqi economy lost over $500 million in oil export revenue, and the global oil markets found new reasons to maintain an estimated $8 a barrel "terror premium" on the price of oil (at a cost of $640 million a day to the global economy). However, this was merely one event in a campaign of sabotage that has already cost the Iraqi government over $7 billion in oil revenues and much more in general economic disruption.

To the trained eye, it was also a demonstration that a small team, at a cost of a couple thousand dollars, was able to safely accomplish an attack that generated a rate of return 250,000 times more than the initial investment.

This attack is part of a larger pattern of violence in Iraq. In the summer of 2004, a group that called itself the Mujahideen Corps took two Jordanian truck drivers hostage. It quickly released a video that included interviews with the hostages. On the video, the group demanded that the company the hostages worked for, Daoud and Partners, a catering company that served the U.S. military in Iraq, withdraw from Iraq within seventy-two hours.[1] If not, the hostages would be beheaded. When the news hit Jordan, the father of one of the hostages told the press that if the company didn't comply he would personally "chop off the head" of the company's chief executive officer. Within hours, the company announced that it would depart Iraq. Less than a day later, the meal services in the U.S.-controlled Green Zone in Baghdad were limited to military rations and cold cuts.

A couple days later, at nine-thirty in the morning, a Daewoo sedan drove up to an Iraqi police barracks in

Ba'quba, a city just north of Baghdad. It pulled up along-side a line of recruits seeking jobs with the police and exploded. The explosion shattered glass, destroyed a mini-van full of passengers just behind the sedan, and raked the line of recruits. Sixty-eight people died in the explosion.[2] In an interview with the press just after the explosion, a local taxi driver confided that he *had been* a policeman, but that he left the job because it was too dangerous.

These attacks, like hundreds of others that Iraq suffers monthly, appear random. We're repeatedly told by U.S. military officials that these attacks are part of a wave of disconnected terrorism that is being perpetrated by des-perate "dead enders" or international jihadis. This percep-tion is wrong. These attacks form a very definite, albeit difficult to discern, new pattern of violence: sabotage that targets critical infrastructures and markets rather than a slavish focus on body counts.

The Rising Danger

> We are not bound by any circumstances, or to anybody, and will continue to fight as it is convenient and advantageous to us and by our rules.
>
> —Shamil Basayev, the Chechen commander and mastermind of the Beslan massacre[3]

This new method of warfare offers clear improvements (for our enemies) over traditional terrorism and military insurgency. It offers guerrillas the means to bring a modern nation's economy to its knees and thereby undermine the legitimacy of the state sworn to protect it. Furthermore, it can derail the key drivers of economic globalization: the flow of resources, investment, people, and security. The perpetrators of this new form of warfare, however, aren't really terrorists, because they no longer have terror as their goal or method. A better term might be *global guerrillas,* because they represent a broad-based threat that far exceeds that offered by terrorists or the guerrillas of our past.

Unfortunately, systems sabotage is easy to implement. The tightly interconnected networks of markets and infrastructures at the national and international levels offer guerrillas incredible opportunity. Small attacks can generate a rate of return (measured in economic damage) a millionfold over their costs.

The signs of this shift to aggressive disruption of systems can be seen across Iraq, and results have been stunning. Iraq's economy is in freefall, which undermines the new national government's legitimacy at the very time Iraq needs it most. Electrical power exists a mere eight to twelve hours a day, far less than what is needed to grow economic activity. Iraq's oil exports are less than half of what they were before the war, which starves the national government of the needed revenue for reconstruction and basic government services. The list goes on: unemployment is at 50 percent, corporations are withdrawing, and investment dollars are scarce. Social systems disruption is even setting the stage for civil war.

The innovation of global guerrillas doesn't stop with new methods of warfare; it extends into how the movement is organized. Because of external pressure, global guerrillas have atomized into loose, decentralized networks that are more robust and learn more quickly than traditional hierarchies. Within Iraq, these networks have combined to create a thriving marketplace, a bazaar of violence, if you will, composed of many entrepreneurial groups— each with its own bond (former Baathist, Sunni, Shiite, and so forth), sources of funding, and motivations. The organic mechanism of the bazaar enables these disparate groups to share information and resources. It also enables them to coordinate their actions to swarm vulnerable targets. So far, this new organizational framework has defied the best efforts of the entire U.S. government to defeat it.

The ongoing disaster in Iraq is a demonstration of the validity of this new method of war and a sign of things to come. What is most disturbing about this development is that the methods used by the global guerrillas we see in action in Iraq are spreading over the entire globe. I don't think this development can be stopped. Soon, an interconnected global bazaar of violence will form as guerrillas around the world adopt the model of success in Iraq.

THE PROBLEM WITH STATES

To understand why the state is so vulnerable, we need to dive into its limitations as an organizational type. The state as an organization, in an organizational framework, has been ascendant since the Peace of Westphalia over 350 years ago—a mere blip from a historical vantage point. For most states outside the Western world, this history has been even shorter. Some states have emerged out of the soup of ethnic, religious, and tribal loyalties only recently.

In aggregate, states have extended their reach to control the economy, personal rights, borders, resources, security, laws, infrastructure, education, and health of their citizens. States as a group, despite numerous internecine wars, have been in strict control of the world's destiny either through direct control or through colonization for at least two centuries. In this process of ascent, they have crushed all opposition, from empires to tribal confederations.

That control is coming to an end.

The culprits are globalization and the Internet.[4] This new environment is sweeping aside state power in ways that no army could. States are losing control of their borders, economies, finances, people, and communications. Their mutual dependencies are quickly eliminating any potential for solo action. They are so intertwined that no independent action can be taken without serious repercussions on multiple levels. To further complicate matters, a new competitive force is emerging in this vacuum of state power. Nonstate actors in the form of terrorists, crime syndicates, gangs, and networked tribes are stepping into the breach to lay claim to areas once in the sole control of states. It is this conflict, the war between states and nonstates, that is the basis for the first epochal or long war of this century.

WHAT DO THEY WANT? FAILED STATES

An example of a claim of a nonstate foe—and there will be as many different claims as there are blades of grass—can be seen in the demands of al-Qaeda. Osama bin Laden, as the spokesman for this nonstate group, has clearly articulated through numerous public statements exactly what it wants to accomplish. It isn't the destruction of our way of life, but specific measurable goals. In his book *Imperial Hubris: Why the West Is Losing the War on Terror,* Michael Scheuer (the senior Central Intelligence Agency analyst once in charge of the bin Laden unit) summarizes these articulated goals as:

- A withdrawal of all foreign troops from the holy sites [particularly Saudi Arabia]
- Elimination of support for apostate regimes [the current crop of totalitarian states in the Islamic world]

- A "fair" price for oil [a fixed price much higher than the current one]
- Denial of support for regimes that oppress Muslims [India, China, and particularly Israel][5]

If you look beyond bin Laden's pontifications and into the statements of al-Qaeda's next generation that is fighting in Iraq, however, you get a different perspective. These young men are part of Abu Musab al-Zarqawi's generation, and they are inspired by the idea of a caliphate that will unite all Muslims (and indirectly make these policy goals reality). To most in the West, the caliphate is parsed as an Islamic superstate. To jihadis, it is something else entirely. Michael Ware, *Time* magazine's intrepid bureau chief and a man who has met many in Iraq's insurgency, captures this sentiment best: "Idealistically, they're striving to create or to return to the ultimate Islamic caliphate, where borders dissolve and nation-states cease to exist, and it's one great Muslim world stretching from Spain through North Africa, the Middle East, and all the way down to Indonesia and into parts of Asia."[6]

This feudal vision of the future boils down to disorder—the hollowing out and failure of the nation-state. In postinvasion Iraq, al-Qaeda found welcoming allies in the Baathists. These men also wanted disorder, but only to make the case to Iraq and the world that they should return to power to provide order again. Even the criminal gangs that are often allies of the insurgents wanted a weakened state because it was good for business.

In other places, the stated goals of these nonstate groups are publicly proclaimed to be economic and environmental. If we jet to Nigeria, the claim made by the newly emergent Movement for the Emancipation of the Niger Delta is $1.5 billion in restitution (for environmental damage and

other problems) from Shell Oil to the local state government and the release of militia and local government leaders.[7] In Pakistan, the Balochs are demanding the termination
of the development going into a local port facility and a
greater share of the wealth generated by local natural gas
deposits. The list goes on, but their actions speak louder
than words: they want to take power from the state and
use it to take control of their own economic and social
destiny. In their minds, if the state fails, they win.

From one end of the world to the other, our terrorist
foes want sovereign states to withdraw from their roles as
the primary actors both within and outside their borders.
They would also like us to revise the economic relationship between the state and the population it sees as under
its protection. To them, a failed state provides a way for
them to both survive and thrive.

It doesn't stop with the states of the developing world.
The methods and techniques of disorder have even greater
applicability to the West. In this fight, they will follow us
back from Iraq. According to Ware:

> Among men whom I would meet in 2003, and I would say,
> "What will it take for you to put down your weapons?
> What will end this conflict?" and their answer [was], "For
> the Americans to leave." A year later, I asked one of those
> same men: "You once said to me if the Americans left, your
> war was over. What now, if the Americans leave, what will
> you do?" He looked at me straight back and said, "If the
> Americans leave now, I must follow them wherever they
> go." Every day this war continues, more and more Iraqis
> join the jihad, the holy war, and that is a global fight.[8]

This isn't the first time states have faced and fought
the demands from nonstate entities. The difference is that
this is the first time in modern history that a nonstate
group has the ability to fight a global war and win.

THE BLEEDING EDGE OF MILITARY THEORY

The time has come for the Islamic movements facing a general
crusader offensive to internalize the rules of fourth-generation
warfare. They must consolidate appropriate strategic thought,
and make appropriate military preparations.

—*Al Ansar,* al-Qaeda's newsletter[9]

The ability of nonstate groups to fight states and win isn't
new. States have been fighting nonstate guerrillas led by
people such as George Washington to Mao Tse-tung for
hundreds of years. These wars were over the control of
the state, however. Successful guerrillas fought governments that were too corrupt, distant, or illegitimate to
function. Successful guerrillas used efficiency, discipline,
and greater legitimacy to take control of the apparatus of
governance; in other words, they were conducting a coup
d'état. In each case, the guerrilla movement served the
function of evolutionary renewal within the state's life
cycle. Failed states were picked off by new, more efficient
(though not necessarily ideal) replacements.

The threat posed by al-Qaeda and other emerging
groups is different. It is not at war with us over the replacement of the state but over who controls the power a state
exercises. Al-Qaeda doesn't want to govern Iraq or Saudi
Arabia. It wants to collapse them and exercise power
through feudal relationships in the vacuum created by
their failure. This stance is exemplified by al-Qaeda's relationship with the Taliban in Afghanistan. In 1996, when
Osama bin Laden returned to Afghanistan, he didn't maneuver to gain control or wield power over a newly emerging Islamic state. No, that would have been a uniquely
twentieth-century goal. Instead, he was eager to build a
new type of organization that operated in parallel and in
concert with the Taliban within the same territory.[10]

The Taliban's failure to create viable institutions of the
state was exactly the type of environment bin Laden

needed to build an organization that could wage war globally like a state, without the limitations necessitated by the administration of territory. This new organization, once established, is now in competition with the states as an equal and not as a successor. Organizations that tried this in the past were typically branded as terrorists and were nothing more than a bloody nuisance. What is different today is that an evolutionary leap in the method of warfare has occurred in concert with a decentralization of economic power—the combination of which makes it possible for even extremely small nonstate groups to fight states and possibly win on a regular basis. We are quickly moving from the exception to the rule.

In most cases, capitalist democracies are still stuck within the confines of borders, bureaucracies, and nationalism. Furthermore, the services that they currently offer their citizens are in broad decline. The environment has changed, but states have not. This has set the stage for the development of nonstate groups that represent the needs of minorities (or at a minimum members of the group) that aren't being served by the states to which they belong. Unfortunately for those of us who have done well under the developed world's rules, these groups are now developing a means of warfare that will allow them to not only survive but also *thrive* at the expense of states.

To understand these new methods of warfare, we need to delve into the bleeding edge of military theory. Bear with me here, because the benefits of this exploration will soon become evident.

THE GENERATIONS OF WAR

If we look at warfare over the last 250 years, broad evolutionary changes can be detected. These evolutionary changes were codified into a generational framework by

William Lind et al. in the prescient 1989 article "The Changing Face of War: Into the Fourth Generation."[11]

Lind is the kind of interesting character who makes a most pleasing dinner companion. He's a historian of German military history, and he was one of the architects of a reform movement to bring the U.S. military into the world of maneuver warfare. In some ways, he seems like a person from another time, more at home with Prussian kings than in today's world (in fact, after turning military theory on its head, he's now devoted himself to turn American culture on its head through his Center for Cultural Conservatism). Perhaps this sense of being born in the wrong era is one of the reasons he can so easily see the broad sweeps of military history.

The generational approach Lind et al. developed is an easy way for even the layperson to get a sense of how warfare is evolving. To begin, let's focus on their first three generations of warfare:

1. Mass warfare. The objective: to defeat the enemy by massing more firepower on the field of conflict. Its roots: the Napoleonic War; the U.S. Civil War.
2. Industrial warfare (World War I). The objective: to wear down the opposing state through greater mobilization and firepower. Its roots: the U.S. Civil War.
3. Blitzkrieg (World War II). The objective: to take down an enemy army and state through maneuver, deep penetration, and disruption. Its roots: late World War I infiltration tactics.

The first three generations deal directly with the arc of conflict between states. As states became more powerful (able to mobilize more people and build greater weapons), and as technology progressed and generated new ideas on how to fight wars, the generations of warfare evolved.

The first two generations were about scale and fire-power. Military forces grew in size through greater mobilization of the state's citizens, who were motivated by nationalism. There were also improvements in how military forces were organized to allow them to move faster and mass more quickly. As the power of the nation-state grew through industrialization and bureaucracy, these increases in size reached their apex in World War I. In this war, the improvements in technology of firepower (the machine gun and artillery) negated the power of mobilization. The end result was trench warfare, where young men were mowed down by the firepower of machine guns. In essence, the bigger the army, the bigger the victory. Mass mobilization had reached its zenith.

In World War II, the conflict between states then turned to technology of maneuver to negate the effectiveness of firepower and mass. Enabled by new technologies of air-power and armor, these new maneuver forces preyed on the extensive logistics systems these large armies required for support. If the army of a state was sufficiently well led, maneuver allowed it to quickly penetrate and destroy an enemy state and its army before it had time to react. This strategy used an army's enormity and complexity as a weapon against it.

The ultimate example of this new type of maneuver warfare is General Heinz Guderian's rush across northern France in 1941. In the opening phases of the campaign, he punched through the front lines of the French front in the Ardennes and ranged deeply in the rear of the French army. With barely enough fuel, only handfuls of tanks, and minimal air support, he was able to destroy military checkpoints, cut lines of supply, attack headquarters, and cause general chaos. For the forward-deployed French troops, who were dug in at the front lines facing Germany, this development caused pure fear.

Not only would they not have the resources to fight but also they would be operating without the precious commands from the centralized headquarters. The inevitable result was a collapse of the French front as its troops headed to the rear. Guderian, of course, continued to push his mobile forces all the way to the sea, and to victory.

This change in focus to maneuver warfare led to a more decentralized command and control system where local commanders created, detected, and initiated the exploitation of opportunity. To visualize this, think about how Guderian operated well behind enemy lines. Constant reference to higher headquarters for orders and direction would slow down the tempo of the attack and allow larger armies and states to recover from the attack. This generation now serves as the desired model for the bulk of the world's militaries (there is still debate as to whether the U.S. military has totally embraced third-generation warfare, given that it continues to focus on the "synchronized" firepower and centralized command and control of the second generation).

The Death of Conventional Warfare and the Rise of the Unconventional

Paradoxically, this evolutionary process ultimately ran into an immovable barrier, the "lost" generation of Lind et al.'s framework of interstate conflict: nuclear warfare. The technology of maneuver, scale, *and* firepower reached its ultimate form as a nuclear missile. This weapon provided states with the capacity to overwhelm their enemies in minutes (it takes a sea-based ballistic missile less than ten minutes to hit a target and a land-based missile from Russia thirty minutes to reach the United States). The proliferation of nuclear weapons and the fear of ultimate destruction have nearly eliminated open wars between developed states. Mutual assured destruction has a wonderful way of making people more risk averse.

A second factor that has nearly eliminated conventional war is rapidly growing global economic and social integration. In today's world, states are too interdependent to easily engage in state-versus-state warfare. The economic and social bonds of most states make them too integral to the global community for them to become targets for invasion. (In fact, this argument is most often made in dismissing the potential for a new cold war between the United States and its newest superpower rival: China.) As a result, gaining legitimacy for war has become very hard to accomplish. International organizations, which have slowly been given the sole role of granting legitimacy in warfare, accord it only in the most unusual of circumstances.

Given this background, the two conventional Iraq wars can be seen as anomalies. The first war was possible due to Iraq's lack of nuclear weapons and its willingness to engage in an illegitimate (and ill-conceived) conventional war with its neighbors. These factors trumped Iraq's integration with the global community to allow a legitimate conventional war to expel it from Kuwait. The second war almost didn't happen. The U.S. fear that Iraq was developing nuclear weapons wasn't sufficient to gain a clear mandate for action. Paradoxically, it was Iraq's isolation from the global community, due to sanctions imposed by the West, that may have made it possible for the United States to go to war with it. Aside from opportunistic political posturing, nobody really cared if Iraq was attacked.

The unusual situation of Iraq provides a stark contrast to the situations of North Korea and Iran. Both are considered threats to the global community; however, both are relatively immune from attack. North Korea's nuclear weapons and Iran's importance to the global economic system make any conventional attack on either one extremely difficult if not impossible. For example, any attack against Iran because of fears that it will develop nuclear weapons will result in massive shocks to the global economy. In short, outside of the occasional anomaly, conventional wars are nearly extinct. Most of the United States' recent "wars"—for example, Afghanistan, Somalia, and Kosovo—were actually interventions within unstable states, rather than a conventional war against them.

Because of these factors, most of the conflicts in the latter half of the twentieth century were fought through guerrilla proxy. States have continued to fight, but through nonstate guerrillas that served as surrogates for their own military forces (the conflict in Lebanon from July to August 2006 is an example of Iran and Syria fighting a proxy war against Israel and the United States). We saw this pattern of conflict span the globe from Vietnam to Afghanistan to everything in between during the cold war.

To summarize, guerrilla warfare as it has been practiced throughout the last 250 years has been used as either a means of proxy warfare between states or a means of replacing the state with a more organized and efficient alternative (part of the evolution of the state—as evidenced by the guerrilla wars of national liberation in the United States, Russia, China, and others). Ultimately, by default guerrilla warfare became the dominant form of warfare in the world—nothing else since the advent of intercontinental ballistic missiles in the early 1950s is acceptable as a form of global conflict.

FOURTH-GENERATION WARFARE

Unlike conventional wars of the first three generations, guerrilla wars are primarily moral conflicts. Because the armies of each side typically never meet on the battlefield, there aren't any pivotal moments that decide the war. Under these circumstances, the side that best withstands the conflict's casualties and disruptions is the winner. The key is maintaining moral cohesion.

To get better at destroying the moral cohesion of the enemy, guerrilla warfare and counterinsurgency have improved. The bulk of improvement has been on the side of the guerrillas, however. Unlike early guerrilla wars of the twentieth century, the guerrilla wars we saw in the latter half of the twentieth century were substantially harder to defeat due to a combination of superpower sponsorship and innovations in method (primarily because of the contributions of Mao Tse-tung and Ho Chi Minh).[12] When we saw both advanced technique and state sponsorship as factors in a conflict, in most cases the guerrillas won.

As we progressed into the 1980s and the cold war faded, smaller states began to adopt the use of proxies to fight their enemies as well. A prime example of this is Hezbollah's bombing of the U.S. Marine barracks in Lebanon on October 23, 1983. By using terrorism and terrorist proxies in the form of Hezbollah and other groups, Iran and Syria were able to drive the United States out of Lebanon (on the cheap).

The global adoption of proxy guerrilla and terrorist conflict led Lind et al. to develop a model for the next generation of interstate warfare. This fourth-generation warfare (4GW) codified the use of guerrilla and terrorist proxies as the primary means of warfare between states, large and small. In Lind et al.'s view, 4GW was a method of warfare that allowed the weak forces to defeat the strong. Within the structure of a sponsored proxy conflict, 4GW was seen as a way to waste the strength of the strong—to bleed the target state dry morally and economically. The result is an eternal war that typically ends with the target state's inevitable defeat.

It's obvious why states have had such a hard time fighting 4GW opponents. The tactics used are a blend of techniques that create a complex jujitsu that turns the strengths of a state into weaknesses. 4GW guerrillas do this by not fighting fair, targeting an enemy's society rather than its military, using asymmetrical methods (different weapons and tactics), and using copious amounts of terror.

Another central problem, as the great Israeli military strategist Martin van Creveld contends with great justification, is that when the strong fight the weak, they become weak.

Creveld has a unique perspective. As a military historian and strategist at the Hebrew University in Jerusalem, he has had a ringside seat on the contest between Israel and its enemies. In an attempt to find ways to defend Israel, particularly against the guerrilla and terrorist threat posed by the Palestinians, he delved deeply into military theory. Unfortunately, the results of his theoretical excursions yielded some discouraging conclusions. His first conclusion was that the nation-state, as we know it, is in decline. The second was that warfare is undergoing a transformation to a new form that will be impossible for nation-states to defeat.

Creveld realized that whenever a state takes on a guerrilla movement, it will lose. The reason is that when the strong are seen beating the weak (knocking down doors, roughing up people of interest, and shooting ragtag guerrillas), they are considered to be barbarians. This view, amplified by the media, will eventually eat away at the state's ability to maintain moral cohesion and drastically damage its global image.

As the state's soldiers continue to fight weak foes, they will eventually become as ill disciplined and vicious as the people they are fighting, due to frustration and mirror imaging. For the state, it will likely not only lose the war but also in the process destroy the effectiveness of its army. Citizens lose their feeling of solidarity with the goals of their government when they perceive it to be acting immorally. The massacre at My Lai represents the United States' most significant stumble over this problem (and the recent revelations about the massacre in Haditha in Iraq continue this trend). Frustrated by the Vietcong's ability to blend in among civilians after an attack, a U.S. infantry company descended on a Vietnamese village, laying waste to it and killing hundreds of noncombatants, including the elderly, women, and children. When the massacre was uncovered more than a year later, by Seymour Hersh in the *New York Times* (his exposé on the Abu Ghraib torture scandal in the *New Yorker*[13] may have been, in hindsight, a similar turning point for Iraq), it led to a palpable shift in public sentiment against the war and the government's conduct in it.

As fourth-generation conflict became dominant at the end of the cold war, guerrillas and terrorists were used throughout the world to combat the encroachment of antagonistic states or cause turmoil among those seen as enemies. In some cases, these proxy forces developed into protostates and carved out sections of their host country for their own. Great examples of this include Hezbollah in southern Lebanon, Hamas in Palestine, and the Fuerzas Armadas Revolucionarias de Colombia (Revolutionary Armed Forces of Colombia). Each of these protostates acted like real states in that they provided services to the populations under their control or within their membership base.

Creveld's description of the slow decline of the state didn't fully anticipate how quickly the global environment would change due to the advent of global markets and the

Internet. Within this new environment, the power and legitimacy of nation-states began to descend in a free fall. This
same environment also radically strengthened the hand of
nonstate groups economically. Because of the arrival of this
new technological and structural leverage, these guerrilla
and terrorist movements, which were once the proxy pup-
pets of nation-states, became autonomous. They also took
the opportunity to rewrite the rules of warfare.

AL-QAEDA REWRITES THE RULES

So we are continuing this policy in bleeding America to the
point of bankruptcy. . . . Meaning that every dollar of al-
Qaeda defeated a million dollars (of the U.S.), by the permission of Allah, besides the loss of a huge number of jobs.

—Osama bin Laden[14]

As with the other generational advances in warfare, the
move to the succeeding generation was made possible
through innovation in ideas and technology to take
advantage of changes in the environment (it's the proto-
typical Darwinian struggle). The improvements in technology that made this generational shift didn't occur in
weaponry, however, but rather in the technologies of
global integration. In this new technological environment,
small groups could travel, communicate, finance, and
trade globally without state support. Translated into military terms, this allowed small groups to finance, plan,
supply, and coordinate attacks globally with little regard
for borders, laws, and governments.

In terms of innovation in ideas, our nonstate foes
leveraged the vast body of literature on guerrilla warfare
(in particular Lind et al.'s 4GW) that was developed in the
United States. It isn't unusual that the people who develop
these new theories of warfare live in the countries that

don't benefit from them. Advanced Western military theory has historically provided sustenance to our revisionist foes. For example, the British military theorists J. F. C. Fuller and B. H. Liddell Hart provided the theoretical basis of armored warfare that Heinz Guderian and others, in the nascent German military before World War II, used to formulate the blitzkrieg. So while the image of al-Qaeda strategists squatting in Afghan caves reading Lind et al.'s 4GW theory may be hard to imagine, it shouldn't be any more fantastic than Guderian practicing Fuller's theories with cardboard tanks. Both happened.

The first application (that we in the West really noticed) of global 4GW by an autonomous nonstate group not acting as a proxy of a foreign power was 9/11. In a textbook application of these new mechanisms of war, al-Qaeda used the technologies of global integration and fourth-generational ideas to attack the United States. In fact, not only were the technologies of globalization used to finance, plan, and deploy the attack team, but also the attack itself used our transportation infrastructure as its means of attack. In classic 4GW fashion, the al-Qaeda planners had found a major strength of the United States and turned it into a weakness. The very technologies and infrastructure networks we use to power our state and interconnect with the world were used against us.

Al-Qaeda also (slowly) learned another major lesson of the attack: that an attack on systems can magnify the effect of a small attack into a major global economic event. Because of the impact of systems, a $250,000 attack was converted into an event that cost the United States over $80 billion (some estimates are as high as $500 billion). The extreme productivity enabled by systems disruption creates the potential for nonstate forces to adopt the strategies of maneuver and attrition in addition to those of moral war. The result would be a long war where an almost endless supply of attackers could generate hundreds of millions, potentially billions, in damage. The cumulative effect of these attacks could grind down even the strongest nation-state.

Here's the upshot (take a breath here, have a smoke, or enjoy a sip of your coffee): the use of systems disruption as a method of strategic warfare has the potential to cast the United States in the role that the Soviet Union held during the 1980s—a country driven to bankruptcy by a foe it couldn't compete with economically. We are staring at a future where defeat isn't experienced all at once, but through an inevitable withering away of military, economic, and political power and through wasting conflicts with minor foes.

To understand how nonstate groups can use systems disruption to undermine states, we need to look closely at how it emerged in Iraq.

3

A NEW STRATEGIC
WEAPON

On the morning of August 1, 1990, Iraqi Republican
Guard divisions uncoiled and began to drive southeast toward Kuwait. On August 2, over one hundred thousand men and seven hundred tanks smashed through the
lightly defended outposts on the Kuwaiti border and
headed for the capital. In a matter of days, the campaign
came to an end as Iraqi troops entered the emir's palace.
The calls for help from Kuwait Radio were silenced.

International condemnation swelled, and the United
States protested the illegal invasion of a sovereign nation.
Iraq replied that its forces would soon withdraw pending
elections for a free Kuwait. The reality was more specific.
This was about the control of oil. In one quick strike, Iraq
had gained millions of barrels of oil in additional production. The real fear was that Iraq would continue its operations to seize Saudi Arabia's Ghawar oil field, which is
merely a day's drive from the Kuwait border. If its 5 million barrels a day of oil were taken, the world would be
Iraq's hostage because Saddam Hussein would own a controlling percentage of the world's oil supply.

Flash forward thirteen years. The world is about to enter another oil crisis. This time demand in growth is putting severe pressure on supply.

THE INVASION OF IRAQ

The U.S. invasion of Iraq in 2003 was a risky move. The underlying intent (despite the pretext of the presence of weapons of mass destruction) was to transform the political landscape of the Middle East. The Bush administration's hope was that radical change—the rapid removal of Saddam's regime and through it the collapse of "politics as usual in the Arab world"—and a decisive demonstration of U.S. military supremacy would reduce global terrorism and establish a new rule set for the Middle East.[1] The new rules envisioned included democratic governments (free from nuclear weapons), rich connectivity to the global economy (specifically in Iraq's case, a rapid increase in oil exports through the removal of sanctions), and good relations with the U.S. as the protector of the region (compliant with United States military activity in the region). However, the invasion of Iraq was actually a lesson in the law of unintended consequences.

The rapid defeat of the Iraqi military and the subsequent domination of the country demonstrated the United States' ability to fight and win conventional wars. Shortly thereafter, however, the glow of victory began to fade as evidence of an insurgency emerged. As the number and effectiveness of attacks by this insurgency grew, it became clear that Iraq was exhibiting patterns of conflict similar to the dominant form of warfare during the late twentieth century: the fourth generation. Despite the best efforts of the U.S. military to counter its growth and the lack of a clearly identifiable state sponsor for the violence, the insurgency became a full-scale guerrilla war in 2004.

One of the major factors driving the growth of the insurgency was a new take on a very old method of warfare: systems sabotage. Ongoing and well-planned attacks on Iraq's infrastructure and social networks threw Iraq's reconstruction into chaos, drained legitimacy from the emerging Iraqi state, and cleaved already weak social fault lines. The leverage provided by these networks amplified the impact of any disruption manifold. To understand how the innovation necessary for systems disruption emerged, we need to examine the innovations of the Gulf War.

THE LESSON THE UNITED STATES LEARNED

Gulf lesson one is the value of air power... [it] was right on target from day one.... Our air strikes were the most effective, yet humane, in the history of warfare.

—President George H. W. Bush[2]

The U.S. air campaign against Iraq during the Gulf War exceeded all expectations of success. It was the first air campaign that completely shut down the functions of a semimodern nation-state. While this had been attempted before, most notably in World War II, that attempt was far from this level of effectiveness. The following is a high-level recap of its impact:

- **Oil and gasoline.** Five hundred sorties and 1,200 tons of bombs were used to shut down Iraq's oil and refining system. Eighty percent of its refining capacity was directly affected. The remaining 20 percent was preventively closed to avoid damage. Iraq was left with only those fuel reserves produced before the war.
- **Electricity.** Attacks against Iraqi power production and switching facilities first shut down its effective use and then collapsed the entire system. This shutdown

cascaded throughout the country as systems reliant
on the national grid were forced to depend on unreliable ad hoc power generation.

- **Telecommunications.** The national telephone system was attacked on an ongoing basis. The ability
  to rapidly repair the network, its built-in redun-
  dancy, and its numerous difficult-to-destroy wireless nodes forced the campaign's planners to order a
  series of repeated attacks to maintain the needed
  disruption.
- **Transportation.** Numerous bridges, railroads, and
  roadways were interdicted to prevent the transportation of supplies and the normal functioning of the
  economy. Transportation connections from Baghdad to southeastern sections of Iraq were successfully severed.[3]

By the time the first ground forces entered Kuwait,
Iraq was a hollow husk of a nation-state. All the vital systems necessary to support economic activity and its military were destroyed. As President George H. W. Bush and
the entire world noted, the air campaign was devastatingly effective. The natural inclination was to assume that
airpower was now a decisive instrument of warfare. This
simplistic analysis misses the point, however. The effectiveness of the air campaign wasn't solely attributable to
airpower. The decisive ingredient was systems disruption.

The devastation of Iraq's systems won the war before
the ground invasion confirmed the process. The important
thing to understand is that the method used to accomplish
this systemic collapse—airpower—was one of many ways
to a similar outcome.

To really understand this, we should dive into how the
innovations used in the U.S. air campaign developed
before the Gulf War. The air campaign in the Gulf War

wasn't a random outgrowth of existing strategy. Instead, it was part of a concerted effort by military innovators to transform airpower from a supporting role to a decisive instrument of warfare. Let's explore how it evolved.

EFFECTS-BASED OPERATIONS

Those skilled in war are able to subdue the enemy's army without battle. They capture his cities without assaulting them and over-throw the state without protracted operations.

—Sun Tzu[4]

In the first twenty-four hours of the air campaign of the Gulf War, 152 different targets were hit—a number larger than the entire eight the Air Force hit in 1942 and 1943 combined, and more separate target air attacks in twenty-four hours than at any time in the history of warfare.[5] The results of this first day and of subsequent days of similar levels of attacks were, needless to say, devastating. However, the reasons for the success of this air campaign can't be found merely in the number of sorties or targets hit; they lie deeper in the theories of warfare and technologies used to achieve success.

The roots of this air campaign began before World War II with the theories of the military thinkers Giulio Douhet (Italy), William Mitchell (United States), and Arthur Tedder (United Kingdom). They advocated the use of airpower to undermine an enemy's capacity and will to fight. However, both theoretical claims fell short when they were applied in World War II:

1. The technology of air warfare was still in its infancy. For example, only 20 percent of the bombs dropped in World War II came within a thousand feet of the intended target.[6] As a result, a massive number of aircraft sorties (at huge cost) were needed to merely

damage a target, let alone incapacitate it. Postwar bombing surveys showed that the Germans were able to both develop countermeasures to Allied strategic bombing and steadily increase production throughout the war.

2. The carpet bombing of civilians increased rather than lessened the Germans' moral resolve. With civilians being killed behind them, soldiers at the front were even more determined to fight than ever before. We can see the effect of these campaigns on today's attitudes. Bombing civilians to destroy their morale is now considered terrorism.

This ineffectual legacy didn't leave the planners of the Gulf War's air campaign deterred. The arrival of new technologies of firepower and maneuver allowed them to realize some of the initial enthusiasm for airpower these early thinkers had envisioned. These technologies included:

- **Precision-guided munitions.** Computer-assisted bombs that hit targets with a very high degree of accuracy. These bombs both minimized the number of aircraft sorties needed to strike a target and reduced the damage necessary to incapacitate it.
- **Stealth.** Technology that made aircraft nearly invisible to radar and other forms of detection. This technology allowed aircraft to maneuver unmolested in enemy rear areas. It also eliminated the need to send aircraft to defend the bombers from attack and limited the need for preattack "softening up" of air defenses. Stealth technology is synergistic with precision-guided munitions.
- **A modern target.** Iraq is a semimodern state, unlike most of our foes over the previous fifty years. Bombers used against Iraq wouldn't be forced to decimate tracks of jungle in the hope of finding a

target. Iraq had a complete and complex infrastructure network. This embedded technology provided the opportunity for exploitation.

Because of the limitation of earlier airpower technologies, traditional air-planning efforts were focused on the complete destruction of the target, usually through the application of massive amounts of firepower (in this case, ton after ton of bombs delivered by aircraft). With new technologies of firepower and maneuver to fuel their efforts, the Gulf War's air planners were able to develop a new approach to aerial bombardment. This approach focused on the disruption of an enemy through maneuver (stealth) and the precise application of firepower (precision-guided munitions) instead of on massive firepower alone. With this new approach, air units were now able to create levels of disruption and confusion similar to that which was previously only achievable by armored units (tanks). Let's look at the theoretical underpinnings of this approach to gain more insight into its implications.

The U.S. air campaign during the Gulf War was built on the theory that the precise targeting of critical nodes in Iraq's infrastructure—electricity, gasoline, oil, communications, transportation, and other systems—could force the Iraqi state into dysfunction and collapse. The planners further realized that to measure the success of this approach, the planning team would need to focus on the effects of their bombing effort on the targeted systems and not the percentage of the systems that were destroyed. This approach was named *effects-based operations* (EBO). The following is a great example of EBO thinking from Brigadier General David A. Deptula, one of the airpower planners during the Gulf War:

> On February 15, 1991, the Iraq target-planning cell received a report on the progress of the air campaign in accomplishing

its target set objectives. Because all the targets in the primary and secondary electric target set were not destroyed or damaged to a specific percentage, the analysis concluded the objective had not been met. In actuality, the electric system was not operating in Baghdad, and the power grid in the rest of the country was not much better off. The effect desired in attacking this system was not destruction of each of the electric sites, it was to temporarily stop the production of electricity in certain areas of Iraq. The planning cell knew the operating status of the Iraqi electric grid and had already reduced strikes against electric sites to *maintenance* levels. The determinant of whether to plan a strike on an individual site was whether the electric system was operating in the area of interest, not the level of damage or lack thereof to an individual site.[7]

This thinking brought airpower theory to a new level of optimization: small and precise attacks made by exceedingly maneuverable forces could (with few casualties) quickly eliminate (in days) the ability of an enemy army and state to function. The flexibility of this technique allowed the war planners to manage the effects of system disruption to create specific outcomes.

In the case of the Gulf War, the desired effect was to prevent Iraq from providing supplies, command, and control to its forces deployed in Kuwait (this should sound similar to what Heinz Guderian did to the French). While Iraq was incapacitated by air strikes, its forces were ejected from Kuwait with minimal casualties in a short ground campaign. This effect was achieved decisively and rivaled the levels of disorientation, disruption, and systems overload normally achieved only through armored encirclements in third-generation maneuver warfare (despite the collective groans of ground warfare enthusiasts).

As a method of attrition (a wearing down of the enemy's economy and will to resist), the air campaign was less effective. The campaign did not last long enough to have a decisive economic impact. Also, there is reason to believe that if the air campaign had continued, the Iraqis would have been able to develop work-arounds to mitigate the effects of U.S. targeting.

As a method of moral conflict, this air campaign had moderate success. It was relatively "clean." The precise targeting of infrastructure minimized the collateral damage to civilian populations and stood in stark contrast to the exceedingly bloody bombing campaigns of World War II. This reality was complemented by an effective media censorship effort that eliminated all pictures of dead or dying Iraqis. The air campaign naturally won plaudits from the world, increased the moral standing of the United States, and reduced tensions at home (a tactical moral victory). It also led to the revolt of major sections of the Iraqi population (another tactical moral victory).

The EBO air strategy was repeated again in Iraq in 2003 in a more limited form for a different outcome. The Iraqi state was again incapacitated, but careful attention was paid to the limitation of damage to critical infrastructure to aid reconstruction. Despite this limitation, Iraq's systems were again forced into failure, and the country's leadership was plunged into isolation. The ground campaign to seize control of Iraq flowed fairly smoothly from start to finish, and the country was taken relatively intact.

Unfortunately, the developers of this new method of attack failed to understand that this innovation in airpower has limited applicability. Outside of Iraq, the potential for another conventional conflict between the United States and another state where this new method of warfare can be used is nearly nonexistent. The combination of the proliferation of nuclear weapons and global integration has wiped the slate clean of enemy states with which we can go to war. As a reminder, both Iran and North

Korea, two of the few remaining states with which we have significant problems, are either too important to the global economy (Iran's oil) or too dangerous (North Korea's nukes) to ever attack.

Additionally, and perhaps more important, the law of unintended consequences went into effect in Iraq during the second war. The lessons learned by Saddam in his bunker at ground zero of the air campaign were very different from those being touted by the West's leadership. To him, systems disruption had a bright future as part of a fourth-generation war (4GW).

SADDAM'S LESSON

In Saddam's last ministers' meeting, convened in late March 2003 just before the war began, he told the attendees at least three times, "resist one week and after that I will take over."

—Charles Duelfer[8]

Because war is a contest of minds, "innovation happens," and even someone as generally incompetent as Saddam can occasionally get things right if they fall within his area of expertise. The complete destruction of Iraq's infrastructure during the Gulf War had a profound impact on Saddam's planning process for the next war. To demonstrate this, let's begin with Saddam's lessons from the Gulf War.

The EB air campaign successfully isolated Saddam and his leadership within Baghdad. The entire Iraqi economy was incapacitated. It was unable to use the electricity, fuel, water, and transportation networks necessary for basic operations or military resupply. Strikes on communications and transportation networks isolated military units from central command authority. As many military organizations do in this type of situation, they simply disintegrated as men returned home. The country's urban areas fell into disarray because of shortages. That, plus the power vacuum created by the lack of communication and the disintegration of deployed Iraqi units, led the Shiite majorities in the southeastern part of the country to revolt. Saddam's country was falling apart while it was being attacked, and he was unable to command anybody but those within his immediate vicinity to stop it. It was a tyrant's worst nightmare.

Due to this disruption, Iraq's military defeat in Kuwait was preordained. It was easy prey for U.S. firepower and maneuver. Not only was there a substantial mismatch in weaponry but there was also a gulf in training. Saddam's army was not even in the same century as the United States' when it came to fighting conventional wars. In fact, when the United States attacked, Saddam's military was fighting a second-generation war (right out of World War I) complete with trench lines.

Iraqi forces were deployed in long trench lines and bunkers along the southern Iraqi border. Tanks were dug in to protect them (ineffectively) from air strikes and to provide artillery support. When the U.S. military did strike, it didn't attack these lines frontally. Rather, it drove across the undifferentiated desert of western Kuwait in a sweeping arc until it flanked the Iraqi trench line. Armed with bulldozers, U.S. troops drove down the trench lines and collapsed the soft sand of the trench walls onto the Iraqi soldiers. Over seventy miles of trench lines were destroyed in this fashion, and an untold number of Iraqi troops were buried in their own defensive works. When Iraqi commanders were captured, they marveled that the U.S. armor was able to traverse the trackless western desert with such precision. The answer U.S. commanders provided was to hold up a handheld global positioning system receiver. This device, they explained, enabled the user to determine his location down to a meter. The Iraqi commanders marveled, "Do all your generals have this?" The reply, "No, every tank has one."[9] The contrast of effectiveness couldn't have been starker.

The impact of these lessons clearly had a major effect on Saddam's planning for a second invasion. Saddam's military understood that in any future engagement, its military would lose any conventional war with the United States both quickly and badly. Given what we can discern (as seen in the *Duelfer Report*[10]) from the interwar period, Saddam's planning team decided to leapfrog third-generation warfare (maneuver warfare) to build the infrastructure necessary for a defense based on 4GW: a guerrilla war.

The defense plan first took form with the establishment of the Fedayeen Saddam (Saddam's Men of Sacrifice) in 1995. This irregular force—composed of men from loyal areas, tribes, and ethnicity—initially served as a personal army for Saddam's son Uday. Over time, it was transformed from a simple collection of thugs to an effective guerrilla force. To supply the Fedayeen and other irregular units with the weapons and supplies after the government fell, Saddam repeatedly ordered his military commanders to stash weapons in the countryside (including farms and homes) between August 2002 and January 2003.

The last step in the process was to select a guerrilla strategy to use. A rural insurgency was certainly out of the question. The terrain (a lack of inaccessible mountains), the high level of urbanization in Iraq, and the lack of broad support among the populace were not conducive to this option. Instead, an urban swarm strategy was selected. First, small teams of guerrillas embedded themselves within Iraq's urban environments to conduct attacks to destabilize the government and inflict casualties on U.S.

forces. Second, Saddam drew on the lessons of the U.S. air campaign to build a strategy of systems disruption to delegitimize the U.S. occupation. His apparent hope was that the denial of critical services and its resulting chaos would improve support for "the good old days" of his regime. To accomplish this, he borrowed heavily on the systems disruption techniques developed by U.S. air planners in the Gulf War and on the methods developed by Chechen guerrillas in their conflict with Russia.

During their wars with Chechen guerrillas, the Russians came out of the conflict the worse for wear. Chechen teams ambushed and decimated Russian armor columns in close combat during the first invasion of Grozny. During the second invasion of Grozny, Russian forces adapted and improved their use of dismounted troops to secure structures before the tanks arrived. This led to the expulsion of Chechen guerrillas from the city and their retreat to the mountains. From 2001 on, the Chechens began a campaign of infrastructure sabotage and selective engagements with Russian forces and their proxies. In one four-day period, they destroyed 300 wells through sabotage and theft. This effort cost the Russian government an estimated $50 million a year and supplied the guerrillas with much-needed financing. It is this final evolutionary step in this conflict—systems sabotage—that proved to be the lesson that Saddam could apply to Iraq.

INFRASTRUCTURE AS A WEAPON

During the Gulf War, the thick plumes of smoke from burning oil wells turned the sun into an afterthought even at noontime in the Kuwaiti desert. From the perspective of satellites, the plumes of smoke from the burning wellheads in Kuwait and southern Iraq stretched deep into the

Persian Gulf and Saudi Arabia with the prevailing south-east winds. For those on the ground, it looked like hell on earth.

As a military technique, this method was basically useless. It shows, however, that Saddam's leadership team understood the use of infrastructure as a weapon of war by setting Kuwait's oil fields ablaze and pumping oil into the Persian Gulf. While these events were ecological disasters, they were clearly not effective as a means of warfare, as even the most simplistic postwar analysis would have demonstrated. In contrast, any postwar analysis would have easily shown how the U.S. air campaign was able to shut down the Iraqi state through small, precise, and mobile attacks on critical infrastructure. To capitalize on this strategy of systems disruption for a second invasion, Saddam's teams of guerrillas were built, deployed, provided with data such as maps, and ordered to attack infrastructure when able.

To its credit, the U.S. military also learned from the Gulf War—another example of minds in conflict. Those who planned the current war knew that the oil fields and associated infrastructure were vulnerable to mass sabotage as they were in the first war. In anticipation of this, the U.S. invasion force during the early phases of the 2003 invasion specifically focused on the rapid seizure of Iraq's oil fields. Within six days of the start of the invasion, U.S. coalition forces had six hundred wells in their possession. Only six wells were actually sabotaged, and their resulting fires were already in the process of being extinguished.[11]

By April 4, the coalition had 80 to 90 percent of the southern oil production and export facilities under its control. By April 21, one month after the start of the invasion, operations were resumed at the Doura refinery near Baghdad. On April 24, the southern oil fields resumed production, and on April 29, the northern fields (near Kirkuk) joined them. This string of good news was capped by President George W. Bush's declaration on May 1, 2003, that major combat operations had ended.

Saddam's fourth-generation guerrillas formally kicked off their campaign of systems disruption on June 12, 2003, with the sabotage of the Kirkuk-Ceyhan oil pipeline in northern Iraq. The proud new owners of Iraq's oil fields were now about to learn a lesson in how warfare is evolving.

THE MODERN EQUIVALENT OF THE SPANISH CIVIL WAR

The new pattern of sabotage, he said, lays the groundwork for chaos—a deeply resentful populace, the appearance of government ineffectuality, a halt to major business and industrial activities. The second side—the suicide bombings, assassinations and kidnappings—he said, is aimed in large measure at sowing discord among ethnic and religious groups.

—Sabah Kadhim, a senior official of Iraq's Interior Ministry, to the *New York Times*[12]

With the stage set for a confrontation in Iraq, the conflict did something entirely expected: it spun out of control. Given this turn of events, the real question is: Which side is adapting faster to the new environment?

One of the best ways to view the war in Iraq in relation to the emerging long war is to cast it in the role played by the Spanish civil war before World War II. It was, like Iraq, a conflict that drew the primary contestants of the larger conflict to it, like moths to a flame. It also evolved the theory of warfare.

In the 1930s, young men traveled to Spain to fight in this conflict, which served as an extension of their desires for freedom, communist expansion, or fascist dominance (take your pick). As they fought, these young men pushed the realm of warfare into new areas. The result was that the tactics and weapons used during the civil war fore-shadowed the strategies and tactics of World War II. German officers, as members of the revisionist power with the greatest motivation for revenge and change, found new methods of warfare with which they hoped to remake the world.

The most telling example was the German Condor Legion's carpet bombing of Guernica. While earlier theoretical work indicated that airpower could be used to destroy cities, it was far from reality—even the 1921 demonstration by the U.S. airpower strategist William Mitchell that aircraft could be used to sink a battleship was considered a staged event. A whole city was generally considered to be beyond the capabilities of the technology.

German strategists disagreed. They thought that the destruction of cities was not only possible but also that it would be a key ingredient in a new strategy of warfare called *total war* developed by Erich Ludendorff (a German general from World War I). In total war, the machinery of entire states goes to war. Civilians are considered combatants, and their destruction is considered a way to quickly destroy the enemy's capacity for warfare.

Airpower, if it could be harnessed, could be the decisive weapon in this new form of warfare—a rapid and effective way to reach inside an enemy's state, destroy its cities, induce panic in the population, and prevent the mobilization of an enemy's army. All that was needed was a test. To prove this theory correct, the Legion destroyed the city of Guernica in April 1937. By all accounts, Guernica was a not a target with any overt military value. It was an open city of five thousand people of Basque origin. The city didn't even have any air defenses. As a target of a military experimentation, however, it was perfect because it hadn't been damaged by the war.

To Lieutenant Colonel Wolfram von Richthofen (a distant cousin of the famous Red Baron), the commander of the German air units used during the raid, Guernica was a pristine laboratory to test new military technology against theoretical capabilities. His test was carried out during fifteen minutes of bombing by three successive waves of German bombers on the evening of April 27. In only fifteen minutes, over 1,600 civilians (this is the best estimate from multiple sources) were killed and two-thirds of the city was destroyed.

As a measure of the ability of airpower to destroy a city, the attack on Guernica was a huge success. But more than that, it was a laboratory of war that produced a successful new strategy.

If Baghdad is the new Guernica, which side is conducting the experiment?

WHO IS LEARNING MORE IN IRAQ?

If [Abu Musab al-] Zarqawi and [Osama] bin Laden gain control of Iraq, they would create a new training ground for future terrorist attacks. . . . They'd seize oil fields to fund their ambitions.

—President George W. Bush, August 31, 2005[13]

[F]ocus operations on [oil production], especially in Iraq and the Gulf area, since this will cause them to die off.

—Ayman al-Zawahiri, September 2005[14]

The major limitation of any learning environment or learning experience is that you get out of it only what you put into it. Learning doesn't take place magically. You also can't learn if you are unwilling to open your mind to new ideas (that often threaten deeply held positions). This common knowledge is being put into play in Iraq.

The problem with Iraq's proving grounds is that it is likely that only one side is really learning. We can see this in the mismatch of perceptions between the sides fighting this war, captured in the quotes presented at the beginning of this section. To President George W. Bush, this war is about extending democracy and defeating al-Qaeda's grip on the insurgency. As an emblematic representative of the mind-set of the U.S. security establishment, Bush sees al-Qaeda as a combination of a proxy foe (for Iran, Syria, and Saddam's Iraq) and a movement for national liberation. The goal of al-Qaeda, according to the conventional wisdom, is to seize control of Iraq by using terrorism and guerrilla warfare.

For the U.S. forces, the focus has been on finding ways to suppress an insurgency by both allowing the people to embrace democracy and eliminating outside influences. According to traditional counterinsurgency theory, a movement of national liberation and/or proxy terrorism can be quickly undermined through simultaneously holding free and fair elections and eliminating support from external states. All of our learning, to the extent it is really taking place (many within the military community have doubts it is), has been focused on this.

Unfortunately, al-Qaeda isn't a proxy force. It is an autonomous entity, a nonstate with its own sources of financing and training. It isn't reliant on states for sustenance. An example of how different it is can be seen in the movement's financing of development projects in Sudan during the early 1990s. Money flowed in the opposite direction, from nonstate to state. It's not primarily a party for national liberation, either. Even to itself, al-Qaeda is seen more as a movement, an instigator of change, rather than as the primary mechanism for seizing control of a nation-state. In this role, al-Qaeda is a spoiler of order, a mechanism that creates the chaos necessary for change.

In Iraq, al-Qaeda is nothing other than a minor player in a larger movement. Our focus on al-Qaeda to the exclusion of the greater part of the insurgency is a disastrous mismatch. It is almost as if the United States and the insurgents are fighting two different wars.

The insurgency's learning goals in Iraq are completely different from our own. It is focused on how to disrupt or spoil the evolving political order rather than to replace it.

DISRUPTING OIL PRODUCTION

Oil is the lifeblood of Iraq. It provides the country with the majority of its revenue. There is a general misconception over how much Iraq's oil production is worth, however. Before the war, the Bush administration claimed that Iraqi oil could finance the war and reconstruction. A glance at the facts proves that is far from the case.

Iraq's prewar oil production was approximately 2.5 million barrels a day, and the market price of oil at the time was approximately $35 a barrel. Iraq's oil exports were worth nearly $23 billion a year in revenue. That is less than $1,000 for every man, woman, and child in the country. Even at 2005's price of $65 a barrel, the total exports would have been $50 billion a year, or just over $2,000 a person.

This analysis indicates that Iraqi oil production isn't a golden goose. It needs to operate at nearly full capacity to have any meaningful effect on the country's economy. It also means that even limited disruption can create a situation where the government and its occupiers are starved for the funds they need to rebuild.

Saddam's guerrilla forces naturally began their campaign against the U.S. occupation by disrupting oil production. These efforts have evolved and generated amazing levels of success. Despite the early U.S. success in seizing Iraq's oil assets and billions in investment, guerrilla disruption has kept Iraq's oil production and exports below prewar levels.

In 2003, most attacks were concentrated on the northern pipelines around Kirkuk. Since the northern fields produce one-third of Iraq's potential production, or 1 million barrels a day, the loss of this production capacity has severely limited the system's recovery.

In the spring of 2004, Iraq's global guerrillas began to attack oil facilities near Basra in southern Iraq. Small but devastatingly effective attacks on pipelines in the area have resulted in hundreds of millions of dollars in lost production and export revenue. In contrast to these uncomplicated and inexpensive assaults, a high-stakes bomb-laden speedboat attack on the heavily defended offshore oil delivery platforms near Basra failed to damage the facilities. So, while global guerrillas will occasionally test the defenses of critical facilities, such attacks generally have very negative "feedback loops." Attacks that work will be repeated until they no longer succeed, and then their perpetrators will try out various other tactics until they find a new success. It's that simple.

TURNING OUT THE LIGHTS

> When you lose electricity the country is destroyed, nothing works, all industry is down and terrorist activity is increased.
>
> —Muhsin Shlash, Iraq's electricity minister[15]

Iraq's guerrillas didn't only focus on disrupting the country's oil production. They found that Iraq's power infrastructure was equally vulnerable to attack.

It's important to take a step back for a moment, though, and ask: Why the electrical grid? It's not the most obvious target, according to the old way of thinking. Critics may have accused Americans of trying to steal Iraq's oil, but no one accused them of wanting Iraq's electricity. Also, it's not a true military target, because the U.S. war machine doesn't need Iraqi electricity to run. The direct victims are just regular Iraqi citizens. So why shut it down?

The reconstitution of Iraq's power infrastructure was intended to showcase the coalition's reconstruction efforts. It was also a critical part of the coalition's claim to legitimacy: that it invaded Iraq for the benefit of its people and not for oil. Furthermore, it is a necessary precondition for revival of the Iraqi economy. In fact, Iraqi electrical production is back to roughly preinvasion levels, but it's not stable enough or rising quickly enough to meet the demands that growth is creating.

To stymie this progress, Iraq's global guerrillas have conducted a systematic campaign aimed at critical nodes of the Iraqi power system. They have cut hundreds of high-voltage transmission lines, toppled thousands of electrical towers, disrupted power plant fuel lines, and assaulted Western engineers. As soon as repairs are made, they attack again.

The results have been spectacular. For most of the postinvasion period, output was below prewar levels, and most of the country operated on less than eight hours of power a day. Baghdad, home to 40 percent of the country's population, saw only a couple hours of electricity a day.

The increase in demand has complicated the problem. The relaxation of sanctions has flooded the market with power-hungry consumer goods. As a result, the country's demand for power is nearly twice the current production. As of December 2005, the U.S. military conceded:

- Up to 40 percent of Iraq's electricity (2,800 megawatts) is in a constant state of disruption.
- Thirty-two assaults on contractors were recorded in December (six killed, five wounded, and two kidnapped).

- The attacks have added excessive costs and delays to the reconstruction and repair effort.

This induced failure has had its desired effect. The coalition lost its legitimacy, largely because of its inability to deliver the basic service of electricity. It is reasonable to assume that if Iraq's global guerrillas continue to disrupt power services, future Iraqi governments will suffer the same collapse of legitimacy the coalition did. What good is a government that can't keep your air conditioner on in triple-digit heat? The United Press International correspondent Beth Potter captured the sense of this dissatisfaction in early 2005: "Iraqi voters aren't happy. They don't care that some of the biggest political changes ever to happen in their lifetime are going on in their country. All they know is that the electricity still is off for hours every day, the water doesn't always flow out of the faucets, there are still long gas queues at the stations, and the situation still seems pretty lawless in the streets."[16]

The consequence is that Iraq will continue to operate as a failed state for at least years into the future. The fight goes on. To prevent guerrillas from getting feedback on the results of their attacks, the Iraqi power company has halted the release of figures on daily power production. Unfortunately, this is mostly a futile gesture because there are other ways of getting the information. For example, the amount of power produced by the huge Doura plant in Baghdad can be estimated simply by counting the number of smokestacks in operation.

COERCING CORPORATIONS

[The] work site, which employs some 260 Iraqis, resembles Fort Knox, as one Bechtel employee put it. (Fearing reprisals, the company asked that none of its employees be named, and that no photographs showing landmarks around the compound be taken.) The site is surrounded by high concrete blast walls, and there is a bunker like inner perimeter where project managers work.

—James Glanz, the *New York Times*[17]

Iraq's guerrillas have found another system that is vulnerable to attack. This is the free movement of corporate employees across borders, particularly the movement of talent from developed countries to developing countries that need it. Iraq's global guerrillas are refining their use of hostages and assassinations as a means of coercion to manipulate this flow.

This strategy became clear when the late Abdul Aziz al-Muqrin's Saudi guerrillas beheaded the American engineer Paul Johnson in Saudi Arabia on June 12, 2004 (which also reflects the spread of these methods beyond Iraq). Al-Muqrin justified the hostage taking and eventual beheading by claiming he was attacking Halliburton. Even though Johnson worked for Lockheed Martin, al-Muqrin and Islamic guerrillas in general believe that all companies providing outsourced support services to the Saudi and U.S. governments fall under the Halliburton label.

Focusing on Halliburton is in line with global guerrilla strategy. It turns the strengths of efficient outsourcing (used to allow the U.S. military to enable its troops to focus on war fighting) into a weakness. The market for outsourced services provided by Western and associated companies is critical to the reconstruction of Iraq, the logistics of the U.S. military, and the operation of critical infrastructure in Saudi Arabia. It's our "soft underbelly." Because these services form a market network, global guerrillas can use the dynamics of the marketplace to amplify the impact of their attacks.

Although they may seem haphazard, the endless series of hostage dramas and assaults on contractors in Iraq form a pattern. They are aimed at the fault lines in the outsourced services market. This pattern is quickly being copied by a rapidly proliferating number of groups that swarm on these soft targets. Global guerrillas are using the following methods to disrupt this market by influencing the psychology of:

- **Multinational companies.** Assaults on employees in Saudi Arabia forced the engineering company ABB to withdraw its employees. Many other companies such as Siemens, Tekhnopromexport, GE, and others have followed suit.
- **Nations.** The attacks in Saudi Arabia targeting Americans caused the U.S. government to urge that all Americans leave the country. Similar attacks on South Korean, Chinese, and Russian employees resulted in government-pressured evacuations of workers of those nationalities from Iraq.
- **Individuals.** Lear Siegler Services typically has had success hiring mechanics for high-paying jobs in Iraq. Beheadings and seemingly random assassinations of Western employees in Iraq have changed the dynamic. At a recent job fair in North Carolina for jobs in Iraq, nobody showed up. "We thought we would have one hundred people waiting for us this morning," said John Bednar, a recruiting manager.

The ongoing attacks against these companies and their employees are increasingly undermining the operation of the market for outsourced services. In large part, this is due to the internal reaction of the marketplace to these systemic insults. Again, we see an example of the leverage provided by global guerrilla methods. These reactions include:

- **Higher transaction costs.** Approximately a quarter (although as of this writing reports indicate that this may have risen to as high as half) of all reconstruction expenditures are now for private security services to protect employees (an effect that will be measured in billions of dollars).
- **Supply chaos.** On August 16, 2004, a Turkish trucker was killed and his rig was set on fire as he sought to deliver bottled water to a U.S. military unit based in Iraq. Critical parts, military supplies, and food have been interdicted on Iraq's unsafe roads.
- **Departures of key people.** The loss of key engineers, through departures or injury and death due to attacks, has left critical projects in Iraq's electricity reconstruction in piles of parts on the floor.

The fact that the vast majority of Iraq's reconstruction funds have yielded little in terms of results shows that these attacks have worked.

SECURITY MARKET MELTDOWN

In 2005, the U.S. focus in Iraq was on building an Iraqi security system that could maintain order. Let's first look at this effort up until 2005. During the period between the end of the invasion and the end of 2004, the United States was able to assemble a large military and police force by hiring anyone who was interested. Because there weren't any other jobs available, the demand for a security job was relatively high. The number of men in uniform ballooned.

Unfortunately, the United States spent little time on training and vetting this force. Instead, it focused on running search and destroy missions against Iraqi guerrillas. The Iraqi military force looked great on paper and to external observers, but this meant little until it was tested. By contrast, the guerrillas were working hard to systematically undermine the development of this force.

The test of which side had done the better job came with the siege of Al-Fallujah. Here's what happened:

- **Guerrilla attacks fractured morale.** Hundreds of attacks, including high-profile mass assassinations, shook the Iraqi security system to its core. The result was a 50 percent attrition rate within Iraqi National Guard groups.

- **Iraqi troops failed to engage.** In a crucial test of the battle readiness of Iraqi units, they failed. In the twenty-four hours before the attack on Al-Fallujah, 100 of the remaining 425 men in Iraq's best-trained battalion, normally 850 men, headed for the hills. The only troops that remained were reconstituted Kurdish Peshmergas. American troops were left to take the city solo.

- **General collapse.** While the United States was engaged in reducing Al-Fallujah, Iraq's guerrillas conducted devastating attacks on Iraqi forces (mostly against the police, given that the National Guard had already been gutted) across Sunni Iraq. The impact of these attacks led most of the rest of the Iraqi security system to fall apart. For example, attacks on multiple police stations in Mosul resulted in the scattering of thousands of policemen. The commander was fired and there are reports of policemen switching sides. This was repeated across Sunni Iraq. Total policemen on hand in Iraq dropped from 84,900 to 43,900 between August and October 2004.

With Iraq's security system in a free fall at the end of 2004, the U.S. military radically reversed its course. The ongoing crisis of the Iraqi state's legitimacy had to be reversed. The interim Iraqi government, because of ongoing attacks on infrastructure, had been unable to deliver the basic services required to legitimatize the government. Iraq was in a general economic collapse.

To increase the legitimacy of the Iraqi government, elections were held. Despite the bump in legitimacy these elections provided, it was soon dissipated for the same reasons listed earlier: it couldn't deliver economic progress. Without broad legitimacy to fuel recruitment and a willingness to die to protect the government, U.S. options were limited. The U.S. military had two choices: it could return Iraq to the now discredited market-based security system (using money as the main means of recruiting forces), or it could do something different.

With so few people willing to risk their lives to protect a new Iraq, the U.S. military decided to recruit and train ethnic and religious paramilitaries. These loyalist paramilitaries quickly filled the ranks, with troops motivated by their loyalty to their ethnicity and religion.

FIGHTING FIRE WITH FIRE

> The Iraqis I met while I was with the Marines were angry about the lack of basic utilities. . . . Iraqis can't understand how a country can overthrow their hated dictator, but can't get the water running.
>
> —Robert Kaplan, *Atlantic Unbound*[18]

In 2005, with Iraq's security system in a slow rebuilding effort based on alternative loyalties, and its economy in ruins, the United States had little left to do except control the chaos and exit the country (before it exploded into civil war).

The essence of a controlled chaos exit solution I was arguing for (as terrible as this sounds) was for the United

States to continue to focus its efforts on building up the forces of loyalist paramilitaries from the Shiite and Kurdish ranks. Of course, this approach should feel familiar because it has been the secret sauce of U.S. counterinsurgency efforts in the post-Vietnam era.

Though many still argue about the worthiness of the cause, the United States has successfully used paramilitary proxies to combat communist insurgencies in Honduras, Nicaragua, and El Salvador. Most recently, the United States used one in Colombia to fight a combination of communism and drug cartel activity. There are three main reasons to use loyalist paramilitaries in Iraq:

- **Loyalty.** Unlike the generic Iraqi forces, paramilitaries draw on tribal, ethnic, and religious loyalties. Close-knit units can be formed on the basis of these long-standing relationships. This loyalty radically increases their unit cohesion.
- **Rapid ramp-up.** These former militia members require much less training than raw recruits (particularly because many of them have had formal training elsewhere).
- **Effectiveness.** Decentralized paramilitaries have a well-deserved reputation for effectiveness. They innovate rapidly and can draw on the same sources of strength available to the insurgents.

I argued in October 2004 that as these paramilitaries stood up, U.S. troops would be able to make a withdrawal. The paramilitaries could have quickly eradicated insurgent activity in areas given to them to control. Unfortunately, a reliance on uniformed paramilitaries always comes with downsides:

- **Institutionalized corruption.** As we have found with the paramilitaries in Central and South America, these forces often involve themselves in illegal activities. For example, Autodefensas Unidas de Colombia (AUC; United Self-Defense Forces of Colombia) is heavily involved in the drug trade. To keep the AUC in line, the government needs to turn a blind eye to this corruption.

- **Human rights abuses.** As we have seen with the recent disclosure that Iraq's Interior Ministry is running secret torture chambers, human rights abuses will proliferate under this system. The reason is that these forces operate within the same rule sets used by the guerrillas they are fighting, such as assassinations, hostage taking, torture, and so forth.

- **Long-term instability.** While the paramilitary militias and their uniformed counterparts will be able to put a lid on the growth of the insurgency, they will not be able to eradicate it. This means that the best we can hope for is ongoing controlled chaos. The worst is that these forces will form the basis for a civil war.

- **Blowback.** As we have seen with our experience in Afghanistan, the use of paramilitaries may result in the development of future enemies. In Iraq, this will certainly be the case.

THE WINDOW SLAMS SHUT

Unfortunately, the United States didn't take advantage of the opportunity to withdraw during 2005 or 2006. Decision makers mistook the controlled chaos enabled by the use of militias for progress toward their maximal goals in the country. That illusion officially ended with the attack on the Samarra mosque (a form of social system disruption, likely a coup de grâce by Abu Musab al-Zarqawi).

After that event, the fragile structure of the system flew out of control as Shiite militias began to target Sunnis.

The United States is now caught between the militias and the guerrillas, and the situation will continue to deteriorate.

Here's one potential bad scenario for how this will play out: deeper entrenchment inside U.S. bases (to limit casualties) and pledges of neutrality (from former Secretary of Defense Donald Rumsfeld) will prove hollow. Ongoing ethnic slaughter will force U.S. intervention to curtail the militias. Inevitably, this will increase tensions with the militias and quickly spin out of control. Military and police units sent to confront the militias will melt down (again) because of conflicting loyalties. Several large battles with militias will sharply drive up U.S. casualties (otherwise, casualties will remain low as the United States stays inside its bases). Supply lines to U.S. bases from Kuwait will be cut. Protesters will march on U.S. bases to demand a withdrawal. Oil production in southern Iraq will be cut (again), bringing Iraqi oil exports to a halt. Meanwhile, the government will continue its ineffectual debate within the Green Zone, a debate that is as irrelevant to the reality of the country as ever. Unable to function in the mounting chaos and facing a collapse in public support for the war, the U.S. military will be forced to withdraw in haste.

Regardless of whether this is the scenario or not, the U.S. withdrawal from Iraq will be ugly.

NEXT STOP: THE WORLD

The United States has had trouble building a security force in Iraq because a cause must have two things going for it to attract a loyal army: it has to be worth fighting and dying for, and the army has to have a chance of winning. Of course, the situation in Iraq fell short. Instead, U.S. military officials found soldiers when they shifted the cause from a united, modern democratic Iraq to securing the country on behalf of ethnic and tribal rivalries.

In the past, winning meant having the largest army. That isn't true anymore. Now, with new forms of warfare, any small group can successfully wage war. With simpler and more appealing goals, almost any cause can raise an army. And they will.

Part II

GLOBAL GUERRILLAS

4

THE LONG TAIL OF
WARFARE EMERGES

In 1618, when Ferdinand II, the Holy Roman Emperor, assumed control of Bohemia, he sent two Catholic counselors to his new acquisition. Bohemian Calvinists reacted by seizing the counselors and throwing them out a palace window to their deaths. This act of terrorism marked the start of the Thirty Years' War, which plunged the center of Europe into chaos.

The Thirty Years' War began as a conflict over religion that drew on the feudal relationships between petty princes and powerful monarchs. As the war continued, the small provinces and kingdoms that had kept European warfare a limited and fragmented feudal affair were ground down by wave after wave of successive invasions by the nascent states of Denmark, Sweden, and France, as well as by counterinvasions by the Habsburgs under the leadership of mercenary entrepreneurs such as Johann Tserclaes, the Count of Tilly, and Albrecht Wallenstein.

In this total war (a war of incredible scale and destruction that considers civilians combatants), the large states were nearly the only entities left intact—only they had the ability to fight at this level and survive it. Their dominance was then codified with the Peace of Westphalia that ended the conflict. In this peace, the basis for the state system that we see today was established. The state's sovereignty over religion (and all else) was in the process of ascendancy. Each successive war since then saw an increase in state control.

Now, after nearly four hundred years of dominance, the primacy of state sovereignty is being put to a test.

In Iraq and in other zones of conflict, we see the stirrings of the reverse of the Thirty Years' War—long and bloody conflict that may be the high watermark of the state. Like its predecessor nearly four hundred years ago, Iraq's war has taken the guise of religious overtones. Sunnis and Shiites routinely kill one another in religious cleansing incidents, which are demarcated by the discovery of the battered corpses of unknown men.

Holy warriors blow themselves up in an attempt at martyrdom, and the armies of the United States and the United Kingdom are routinely referred to as Christian crusaders. However, this religiosity is only a veneer on the conflict despite the allure of categorizing this a "clash of civilizations." The real roots of Iraq and other emergent global conflicts are much more complex. This new "Thirty Years' War" is being defined by the limits on state power and the rise of mechanisms that power the decentralization of warfare.

Perhaps al-Qaeda is subconsciously in tune with this shift. Its vision of an Islamic state isn't a state in the sense that you and I think of it. It is a loose feudal state similar to the caliphate that ruled the Middle East a thousand years ago. It's a decentralized system of affiliation and deference.

Constraints on Total War

On the evening of February 2, 1982, Hafez Assad, the Syrian dictator, initiated the bombardment of the Syrian city of Hama. The city had become a hotbed of opposition to the regime and the home to the Muslim Brotherhood, an Islamic fundamentalist movement. To combat this threat, Assad took a page out of the state's playbook for success: total war. He surrounded the city with tanks and artillery and then blew up the exits from the city with air strikes so no one could escape.

The intense bombardment lasted for days and was followed up with house-to-house searches, executions, and bulldozers. Twenty thousand people died (some estimates are as high as forty thousand). The event put an end to the insurrection of the Muslim Brotherhood. The international outcry was intense, however. It branded the state's actions as state-sponsored terrorism. Syria's actions demarcate the end of a state's ability to use its power to adopt total war as a means to eliminate opposition.

A key factor driving the decentralization of warfare (and potentially the reverse of the gains made in the Thirty Years' War) is that the total war that ushered in the dominance of the state is now nearly obsolete. The wars that states, at least western ones, can wage today are tightly constrained affairs. A major reason for this is that the stakes are lower for any given conflict. High-risk wars with other states are extremely rare because of the potential for nuclear holocaust, and as such are fast becoming extinct. The upshot of this is that wars no longer put developed states in mortal jeopardy.

Today, wars are wars of choice. This means three major factors have changed:

1. **The resources allocated to war will remain limited.** For example, despite the shock of 9/11, the United States didn't reconstitute the draft or marshal the taxation and control of industry necessary to wage total war against al-Qaeda. The war is being fought with limited resources on the margins of American society and economic activity. There is also a constraint on activity posed by the increasingly competitive global economic system. Any state that warps its function to wage war may quickly find itself at the mercy of the global credit markets.

2. **Moral constraints now radically limit military options.** The lack of life-and-death stakes makes it impossible for states to transcend moral boundaries. In the future, wars perpetrated by states will no longer include a Sherman's march to the sea or the firebombing of Tokyo. Civilians and their property are now, to a large degree, off limits. The firestorm in public opinion over the abuse and humiliation of prisoners at Abu Ghraib is a demonstration of what can happen when moral constraints are even eased slightly. The global media are also willing to act as a watchdog for violations of complex moral codes of conduct (in that they are often based on cultural and religious sensitivity). Their role can turn the burning of Afghan Taliban corpses by U.S. troops— which would have been a blip in total war—into incendiary front-page news.

3. **Interdependence drives decision making.** The inability of the United States to act against Iran is an example of how global economic interdependence constrains warfare. The need for Iranian oil and gas has put the country under the protection of China and India. The United States cannot get the authorization it needs from the United Nations to

act against the state for either its support of Iraqi guerrillas or its nuclear program.

The nation-state is now bound up in a straitjacket of constraints. The core of its strength, its ability to marshal resources and take actions that exceed the power of any smaller organization, has been made increasingly impotent. We won't ever see the tens of millions of men under arms like we did in World War II.

In a very definite sense, the cozy and highly regulated market of warfare characterized by wars between state oligopolies is eroding because of these constraints. Furthermore, as we have seen in Iraq, the rise of globalization and the Internet has accelerated the development of nonstate foes. The result is a new, competitive market for warfare more akin to the years before the Thirty Years' War than to our recent past. The participants in this new market are small adroit nonstate competitors and occasional allies—guerrilla/terrorist groups, paramilitaries, and private military companies—and they are in the process of rewriting the rules of warfare.

LONG-TAIL MARKETS

To understand what happens to traditional markets when they are hit squarely by new competition enabled by a combination of the Internet and globalization, we need to turn our attention to the work of Chris Anderson. Anderson, the editor of *Wired* magazine, defines the characteristic of what he calls *long-tail markets*.

To use one of his best-known examples, think of your neighborhood Barnes and Noble superstore, which carries about 130,000 titles. By contrast, Amazon has a nearly limitless number of titles, so guess how much of its sales comes from books outside that top 130,000? One percent? Ten percent? A quarter? In fact, more than half of

Amazon's book sales come from outside its top 130,000 titles. Consumers love variety, and if the technology is there to allow them to make informed choices about a massive number of products, they'll all choose different things.

The long-tail idea comes from the concept of a power law. A power law typically defines the relationship between sales (in units) and the number of different products available in an industry segment. In the past, if we graphed this power-law relationship, we would see a few products (hits) with a very high volume of sales quickly dropping off to a finite number of less popular versions of the products. A distribution of last year's popular movies or of automobile sales might look like this. Because of the financial threshold for creating and distributing a new product, most of the total sales come from the top. This power-law curve has a short tail.

Anderson's work shows that the Internet has radically changed the relationship for many types of products that come in a multitude of varieties (like books and music). The sales of niche products are quickly becoming the dominant force in the markets for many product categories—the new tail is both longer and fatter. Whatever product you create, you can now find a customer for it, no matter how small the market. The tail of the power-law curve doesn't drop off—it goes on seemingly indefinitely. This is the long tail.

There are a few reasons why the Internet and globalization have forced this market shift (I will show you shortly why they have applicability to warfare in the twenty-first century):

- **The tools of production have been democratized.** It is now possible for niche producers to develop and make products for much less cost than previously. This is especially true for products with high information content, like highly specific software, home videos, or Web log (blog) posts.

- **The costs of buying niche products are lower.** The unlimited shelf space of online retailers makes it possible to list niche products at nearly zero marginal cost. The cost for listing ten thousand products is nearly the same as listing one hundred thousand.
- **It's easy to find and choose among these niche products.** Tools such as Google and collaborative filters such as Amazon's reviews and recommendations make it easy to find niche products. Nearly any product is just a couple of clicks away.

As this new fat-tail market has emerged, the way firms produce products has changed as well. The old model of lowest-common-denominator product development is slowly going away. Backlist sales are up, and niche-enthusiast-matching sites like eBay, MySpace, and YouTube have become the new thing. In the near future, general-purpose software laden with seemingly useless features and Hollywood films that are made with traditional formulas will give way to more focused products that cater to the needs of niche buyers.

THE LONG TAIL OF IRAQ'S WAR

It's like a gang war, and we're the biggest gang.

—U.S. soldier on patrol in Mosul, Iraq[1]

Iraq's insurgency has developed a long tail similar to what we see in the online retail markets. The insurgency is not a single army with one goal. Instead, it's actually made up of hundreds of small groups (seventy-five of which have been identified) currently operating in Iraq. These groups range from a small family group to large ideologically motivated groups measuring in the thousands. None of these groups is large enough to be considered dominant, and each is motivated to resist the U.S. occupation of Iraq for different reasons. Regardless, we can discern the following broad categories of motivation:

- External Sunni fundamentalism
- Local Sunni fundamentalism
- Saddam loyalists
- Baath loyalists who didn't want Saddam to return
- Sunni nationalists
- Tribal groups
- Criminal gangs
- Shiite fundamentalists

If we graphed the number of guerrillas by the number of groups in this volatile Iraqi soup, we would likely see the ideal long-tail distribution—lots of small niche providers of violence. All these groups are in competition, but at the same time they are willing to work together to fight the United States by building a market that advances the fortunes of all.

The development of this long tail of insurgency in Iraq is being driven by factors that are similar to those that transformed the commercial retail markets. These factors include:

- **The decentralization of the tools of warfare.** The costs of conducting warfare are rapidly declining. As we have seen in the Iraqi oil system, systems disruption and the asymmetric nature of vulnerabilities (we have a vulnerable infrastructure; they don't) make it possible for even a small group to create outsize levels of damage. A simple attack that costs in the thousands of dollars can create damage that costs the state hundreds of millions of dollars.

- **Unlimited shelf space.** Technology has made it easier to network with others with your particular obsession, whether it be old episodes of *The Simpsons*, or killing the infidel. Raising an army means finding only a dozen similarly minded people, and it has become easier than ever to find those people.
- **Low barriers to entry.** As we saw in the attacks on the London subways, it's possible for groups that want to join the conflict to act in concert with groups like al-Qaeda. Potential bombers don't need to agree with the leadership, get support from them, or even know them. Conducting their own operation is enough.

POPULATING IRAQ'S LONG-TAIL INSURGENCY

It's too late to stop the trading [in weapons]. There are too many hidden stores of weapons and people are dealing and trading freely.

—Qais Najeeb, an Iraqi smuggler, to
United Press International[2]

The shift to this new long-tail structure hasn't been appreciated by the U.S. military. It still views the insurgency in classic terms. Historically, insurgencies in the fourth-generational mold have been predominately rural and associated with a single-party doctrine. They also grew slowly and deliberately through the extension of a unified command structure.

As a result of this experience, our entire counterinsurgency doctrine reflects a focus on defeating a foe that looks like this. It also colors our analysis. A critical assumption on which we have based our efforts in Iraq is the estimate of the size of the insurgency we are fighting. According to the U.S. military, the Iraqi insurgency has between twelve thousand and twenty thousand members, which likely reflects our bias toward groups that look similar to our historical experience. Our expectation is that they are controlled from the top down and that they share a common set of goals.

Again, according to the U.S. military, however, we are capturing or killing insurgents at a rate of one thousand to three thousand a month, and fourteen thousand insurgents are now being held in U.S. prisons in Iraq. If we accept this math (even though body counts are typically inflated), Iraq's insurgents have suffered a monthly loss rate of over 10 percent for the last two years. If taken in total, the entire insurgency has been destroyed or imprisoned at least once since the invasion. Typically, when an organization suffers this level of losses, we would expect to see a catastrophic falloff in the quality and quantity of attacks. This hasn't happened. In fact, exactly the opposite has happened.

Despite this apparent success, the number of daily attacks by insurgents on coalition forces continues to keep reaching new highs, and the quality of the attacks has also improved with the introduction of new technologies for advanced bombs and new types of targets. By all accounts, the insurgency appears to be strong and getting stronger. The most likely explanation for this is that the estimates we have for the insurgency are fatally flawed. We have likely based our estimates on a model of the insurgency that doesn't fit the current long-tail reality.

To correct this, we should start with a clean slate and build a better estimate. First, we should ask ourselves who has both the capability and the desire to be an insurgent. We also need to appreciate the planning Saddam Hussein's regime put into developing the groundwork for a guerrilla war. Those most capable of being insurgents are the Sunnis with a background in the former Iraqi government, particularly those with some level of military training. These groups were given special training and encouragement before the invasion by Saddam to build guerrilla networks. These groups fall into the following categories:

- The Fedayeen Saddam. A special group of ultraloyal Iraqi irregulars. This group was started by Saddam's son Uday but was later turned into an officially sanctioned guerrilla organization. Estimates of its strength range from 40,000 to as high as 100,000 (which reflects a last-minute buildup before the war).
- Sunni officers in the Iraqi Republican Guard and military. This group is likely at least 175,000 out of a total prewar military force of 700,000 men.
- Members of the secret police (the Mukhabarat) and other internal organizations. Estimates are 100,000. This high number reflects the bias of the Iraqi regime toward internal protection.

At this point, we are starting with a pool of over three hundred thousand men who have the training and the capacity to fight an insurgency. Let's focus next on motivation. Two events demarcate an expansion of the insurgency beyond this trained group. The first was Paul Bremer's disbanding of the Iraqi military. The second was the de-Baathification of the Iraqi state, which most recently was written into the new constitution. Both measures have served to completely alienate those most capable of conducting insurgency, because they are now effectively men without a state or a job. Former generals are now reduced to a pension of $40 a month, and many have turned to driving taxis to supplement their income. Furthermore, it can be argued that this diminishment has been extended, through the ethnic and religious politics of Iraq, to include the entire Sunni population of Iraq. Because of this, we can extend our analysis to include two more groups with the motivation to participate in the insurgency:

- Senior Sunni Baath Party members. The Baath Party had 2 million members before the war. Senior Sunni membership can be estimated to be at least 50,000 if not more.
- Sunni men not in the previously mentioned groups. This is a large group of 1.5 million men out of a total population of 5.2 million Sunnis.

From this pool of potentially motivated and capable participants in the insurgency, we are now ready to make some estimates of the size of the insurgency. A good approach is to use a best, likely, and worst-case estimate for the levels of participation from each of these groups. From these calculations, we should be able to determine the weighted average for the insurgency that reflects a 20 percent weight for the best case (only hard-core members are involved), a 60 percent weight for the likely case (a hard-core base plus a large and extremely active support and auxiliary force), and 20 percent for the worst case (all the previously mentioned plus a very large indirect support infrastructure). The calculation of a weighted average of potential outcomes is a standard approach in analyzing the potential payouts from financial investments with ambiguous outcomes.

If we apply this analysis to these groups, we face, at the very least, 40,000 active insurgents. Counting all the people who could participate depending on political and other factors, the insurgency has the potential to expand to over 300,000. For planning purposes, we should expect to face an active insurgency of over 150,000 members on any given day. This estimate is much, much higher than that presented to U.S. decision makers by the U.S. military. Under this new estimate, the percentage of the insurgency captured or killed every month is approximately 1 percent of the entire decentralized organization. This is a level of losses easily maintainable given historical experience, and it fully explains the ability of the insurgents to increase the number and quality of their attacks.

This estimate also indicates that given our current assumptions and tactics, the U.S. prospects for a successful resolution of the insurgency, even within a decade, are very low to nonexistent. Typically, counterinsurgency requires at least an overwhelming advantage of conventional forces over insurgents (some estimates are as high as 10 or 20 to 1).

We don't have that, because the insurgents outnumber us even if we include both those elements of the Iraqi military that are able to operate without U.S. support and the best-case estimates of attrition we have inflicted. Most important, successful counterinsurgency requires the willing cooperation of the public, or a sizable fraction of them, to identify the insurgents and help locate their hiding areas and bases of operation. Clearly, we do not have this cooperation.

Primary Loyalties: Manufacturing Nonstate Groups

Besides the organic growth of nonstate groups into the gap left by the decline of the state's ability to wage war, global guerrillas have developed a way to manufacture them. These methods provide a way to populate the tail of insurgency and paramilitary ranks with a growing number of participants. The chosen method for accomplishing this is through attacks on systems that provide the bonds of moral cohesion that keep a nation intact.

We can see this in the ongoing guerrilla attacks on symbolic targets (like Shiite mosques), state security forces, and the destruction of vital infrastructure. This produces a combination of economic necessity, outrage, fear, and revenge that pushes people to fall back on their primary loyalties.

A primary loyalty is a form of ancient moral connection that transcends loyalty to the nation-state. These include connections to family, clan, tribe, gang, religion, and ethnicity. These loyalties are reciprocated through the delivery of political goods (economic aid, safety, and more) that the state cannot or will not deliver.

Once the descent to primary loyalties has begun, it creates its own positive feedback. In Iraq, Sunni guerrilla attacks on Shiite civilians and symbolic targets begets Shia militias. These militias kill Sunni civilians and damage Sunni symbolic targets. In parallel, attacks on the fuel and electricity infrastructure force people to look to primary loyalties for economic support. The ongoing need for protection and economic survival creates a cycle that strips the state of any remaining legitimacy. The final result is a descent into civil war or grinding anarchy.

EXPORTING INSURGENCY TO THE WORLD

Still, if the theory holds true, wouldn't we be seeing more of it outside Iraq? The principle that every cause will find its combatants ought to apply worldwide, right? Disturbingly, we're beginning to see it in motion in a variety of global conflicts, from the swamps of the Niger Delta to the mountains of western Pakistan to the beaches of Thailand. In each case, organic guerrilla movements have emerged. All these movements lack any cohesive leadership structure. They are an amalgam of tribal loyalties, criminal gangs, clans, religious groups, and ethnicities.

They are small causes and groups that are finding that they can make a major impact.

THE CAUCASIAN FRONT

Chechen guerrillas have subordinated their units into a larger amorphous entity called the Caucasian Front. Additionally, they have begun to focus on economic targets. A list of assaults in 2004 on Russian infrastructure (compiled by the Jamestown Foundation), with its improvised explosive devices (IEDs) and damaged pipelines, looks like it could be from Iraq:

- February 18, Moscow. Two gas pipelines were blown up with IEDs made from rocket-propelled grenades.
- March 15, Moscow. A power transmission line was severed. A Chechen flag was found at the blast site.
- April 5, Dagestan (southern Russia). The Russian gas export pipeline to Azerbaijan was interdicted for several days.
- April 5, Chechnya. The Baku-Novorossiysk oil pipeline was damaged because of collocation vulnerability with the gas pipeline.
- April 24, Volgograd. The Samara-Lisichansk long-distance pipeline was blown up.
- May 24, Dagestan. The Mazdok-Gazimagomed gas pipeline was damaged.
- June 5, Stavropol. The Baku-Novorossiysk oil pipeline reservoir was bombed.
- July 5, Chechnya. The Mazdok-Gasimagomed pipeline was damaged again.
- November 28, Moscow. A circular gas pipeline was severed.
- December 8, Dagestan. The Russian gas export pipeline to Azerbaijan was blown up.

MEND in Nigeria

Nigeria is an evil entity. . . . I will continue to fight and try to
see that Nigeria dissolves and disintegrates.

—Alhaji Mujahid Dokubo Asari, the leader of the
Niger Delta People's Volunteer Force[3]

The Movement for the Emancipation of the Niger Delta is
a new umbrella movement about which little is known. It
has numerous spokespeople and ties to tribal affiliations
in the Niger Delta. Recent attacks are substantially more
sophisticated than previous efforts, which were typically
either riots, protests, or bunkering gone awry. These new
attacks include:

- Swarm-based maneuvers. The guerrillas are using
  speedboats in the Niger Delta's swamps to quickly
  attack targets in succession. Multiple, highly maneuverable units have kept the government and Shell
  Oil's defensive systems off balance defending the
  sprawling network.
- Radically improved firepower and combat training.
  This new capability allows the guerrillas to over-
  power a combination of Shell's Western-trained private military guards and elite Nigerian units in
  several engagements. One of Shell's private military
  operators was taken hostage in January 2006.
- Effective use of system disruption. Targets have been
  accurately selected to completely shut down production and delay or halt repairs. This is a systematic
  operation. Additionally, the guerrillas are making
  effective use of corporate hostages to coerce both
  the government and the companies involved.

This new level of sophistication, and its explosive
emergence in Nigeria, demonstrates that global guerrilla
methods such as those demonstrated in Iraq have made

the leap to Nigeria. The source of the new capability is still unknown, regardless of its origins. If the pattern of development we have seen in the past is followed, other indigenous groups in Nigeria will quickly adopt the same approach. The result will be widespread open-source warfare that focuses on systems disruption. This will mean the following:

- Massive disruption. Given the capabilities demonstrated, estimates of potential disruption in Nigeria could reach one million barrels of oil a day on average.
- A cash crisis in Nigeria. The country's loss of oil revenue may cause massive instability, which could fuel further conflict. If this is combined with disruption of basic services in the cities, all bets for the future of Nigeria as a cohesive state (even a relatively nonfunctional kleptocracy) are off.
- An accelerated spread of global guerrillas. The successful coercion and (potential) collapse of the Nigerian and corporate status quo will be a strong incentive for other groups to replicate their methods.

As Reuters's Tom Ashby says, "Unlike some previous movements which have fought for outright independence for the delta, which pumps almost all of Nigeria's 2.4 million barrels per day, these militants said they want to stay in Nigeria but with more regional autonomy."[4] My take on this: Again, the essence of many global guerrilla wars won't be to replace or break away from the state, rather, it will be to hollow it out.

THE BALOCHS IN PAKISTAN

Pakistan is facing a global guerrilla insurgency (modeled on the most effective parts of the Iraqi insurgency). Baloch

tribesmen have begun a campaign of systems sabotage in
an effort to gain coercive leverage with Pakistan's government. They have attacked natural gas systems, railways,
phone systems (cell and landline), and electrical grids
across the country (both within and outside their province). Based on the damage reports, these attacks may be
yielding returns on investment (ROIs) of at least 1,000 to
1. If they are able to scale this ROI through the use of network analysis, Pakistan may face major consequences. It
is already calling into question international investment in
the country.

More important, if the actions of the Balochs can disrupt the infrastructure of the rest of Pakistan, a rapid
decline in the delivery of basic goods (core services) will
follow, which could result in the rapid fragmentation of
the country. This would entice other autonomous networks to join in the systems sabotage.

A proposed $4 billion Iran-Pakistan-India natural gas
pipeline system is now in jeopardy. Much of this system
would pass through the province (however, given the
national reach of these guerrillas, it wouldn't matter where
in the country it is located). Pakistan plans to receive up to
$500 million a year in fees from this venture. Delays on
this deal alone could cost Pakistan $42 million a month. If
this is resolved in the short term, and the pipeline is put
into place, a disruption would have a major effect on
India's economy.

ISLAMIC SEPARATISTS IN THAILAND

Over the past year, the Islamic separatist movement has
taken off in southern Thailand after five years of limited
success. Attacks in 2005 were up to twenty a month, three
times the 2004 rate. As with many of the other groups discussed in this chapter, this movement has shown remark-

able innovation in a very short period of time. This innovation includes improvements in weapons, technique, and organization. Recent attacks include systems disruption and advanced bomb-making techniques, such as IEDs. The following is a snippet from the Jamestown Foundation (which focuses on, among other things, Eurasian terrorism) on activity in Thailand in late 2005:

> Further evidence of the mounting threat is found in a new trend demonstrating sophistication and organization in the use of coordinated attacks. On November 2, a series of blasts near electricity poles and a transformer substation detonated at intervals of 10 minutes for over an hour, and resulted in a total loss of power in Narathiwat town. In late October, a similar series of coordinated attacks targeted at least 43 security posts over the three provinces of Pattani, Narathiwat and Yala. In one spate over the night of October 26–27, militants carried out at least 20 attacks, mostly targeting the new civilian militias.[5]

These parallel, regional attacks were made possible through the use of cell phone infrastructure (as happened in Madrid). The attack on the electricity infrastructure was particularly astute because it doubled the amount of leverage provided by infrastructure—particularly because this electricity disruption resulted in a cascading failure that took down the entire system.

To defeat the leverage provided by cell phones, the government responded by controlling access to this critical infrastructure:

- Turning off cell phone service in the affected province during the November 2 attack on the electricity infrastructure. This allowed the government the time necessary to defuse multiple unexploded bombs.
- Forcing prepaid calling card phone users to register their phones in the affected provinces. This is in

progress and affects nearly half a million phones in the area.

- Extending registration of prepaid phone cards to the entire country. This will likely occur in the next year.

PARAMILITARIES

We are respectful of foreign investment; we have not kidnapped any people from multinationals; we do not resort to terrorism as a regular weapon; we do not kidnap people for purposes of extortion; it is not our aim to destroy the state.

—Carlos Castano, commander of the Autodefensas Unidas de Colombia (AUC; United Self-Defense Forces of Colombia), a right-wing Colombian paramilitary group[6]

While those terrorist groups aim to rob power from the state, some paramilitaries have worked to supplement the state. Though roughly aligned with the state that contains them, they have their own agendas, methods, and networks.

The rise of the role of the market, at the expense of the state, has in many places stretched the state to the breaking point. In no place has this become more evident than in China. The rapid pace of economic growth in the country has radically outpaced the capacity of the government to police it or mitigate its negative effects. The result has been a rapid rise in the number of economic protests from people demanding protection and/or support. Protesters have risen from thirty thousand in 2004 to over seventy thousand in 2005.

China, like almost every other country in the world, has begun to shift from traditional military to a paramilitary approach to control domestic unrest. The experience of the last decades with paramilitary forces indicates that they can act as a protector of the market function within national borders much better than simple police or national militaries. The growth of paramilitary market police has been sudden and rapid.

China has embarked on a program to train and arm well over a million domestic paramilitary forces to maintain domestic order. Paramilitary forces are currently being heavily used in Turkey, Pakistan, Iraq, Lebanon, Russia, and virtually every other country on Earth. Even the United States hasn't been immune. There has been a radical increase in the number of SWAT teams throughout the United States, and the frequency of their use has skyrocketed.

In parallel to the increase of authorized paramilitaries, there has been a grassroots increase in ad hoc militias.

The Minutemen

In the United States, the most famous ad hoc militia is the Minutemen, named after the famous New England patriots who assembled to fight the British redcoats during the American Revolution. Armed to the teeth with semiautomatic weaponry and survival gear, this paramilitary force has formed organically to police the U.S.-Mexican border.

Though many Americans have lamented their existence, few have tried to explain it. Because fear of immigrants has been with the United States since even before its founding, it's worth asking: Why now? The emergence of the Minutemen is a good indication that the nation-state is in decline, even within its strongest member. Russell Morse, writing for the Pacific News Service, captures a snapshot of the militia that is worth recounting. Here, he describes the who, what, and where of their work:

> This is Campo, California—Borderland—an hour east of San Diego, where a handful of volunteers is anchoring a border watch operation. The stretch of rocky desert they patrol is a busy thoroughfare for people coming into the United States from Mexico illegally. Breaks in the border

fence, a network of hidden trails and a series of canyons make the area a safer point of entry for immigrants. . . . Beyond the guns and trucks and high speed chases, though, are idle hours and a group of men who believe they're protecting America, giving their lives to the work, they say, their government refuses to do. Most are ex-military, Vietnam veterans, retirees, unmarried, from rural corners of California who were looking for something to belong to and found it in the desert.[7]

The mix of patriotism and a sense that they are defending a way of life are the motivations behind the growth of the Minutemen. Specific fears they tend to cite are floods of illegal aliens that will take jobs away from Americans, drug smuggling, and the potential that al-Qaeda terrorists will cross the border. They may not have strength in numbers, or a broad agenda, but this is the twenty-first century, so they found one another.

So far, these men have taken a relatively passive role in helping federally sanctioned border patrol agents enforce the law. Here's an example of one of the Minutemen's operations:

> We reach La Gloria Canyon, floating on a dust cloud. . . . Bandit [the call sign of one of the Minutemen] is perched on the edge of a cliff, with binoculars and his radio, still yelling. He tells us that a Border Patrol spotted 13 people who crossed just before sunrise and is in the process of boxing them in. Bandit's job now is to organize his team to seal the southern perimeter so none of the 13 can cross back into Mexico. . . (later) the thirteen immigrants are apprehended and we all head back to camp.[8]

The AUC in Colombia
The AUC was built to defend the interests of rich landowners and multinational corporations. It was given a franchise by the government to fight encroachment by

communist guerrillas such as the Fuerzas Armadas Revolucionarias de Colombia (Revolutionary Armed forces of
Colombia). Recently, there has been a push to disband the
AUC because it appears that the government is increasingly
able to handle its own security. This is complicated, however, by the fact that the AUC members getting amnesty in
the program are heavily involved in the drug trade.

PRIVATE MILITARY COMPANIES

We are not simply a "private security company." We are a
turnkey solution provider for 4th generation warfare.

—From the Web site of Blackwater, a U.S.-based
private military company[9]

Another trend along the same lines as global paramilitary
growth has been the growth in private military companies
(PMCs). These are the rich man's version of the poor man's
paramilitary, and they're undergoing a renaissance in usage.

The rise of private militaries is a throwback to their
historical presence. In most of recorded history, mercenaries have played a prominent role in warfare. Until the
advent of rifles, the highly developed martial skills of the
mercenary set them apart on the battlefield. The skills gap
disappeared with the advent of simple weapons, however.
Soon, the mass conscript armies of nation-states were able
to eliminate them from the battlefields. If we take the long
view, this development was only a recent historical blip.
While the term *mercenary* is still filled with heaps of oppro-
brium, the profession has made a mighty return to legitimacy within the security systems of modern nation-states.

The path of this return is based on two vectors. The
first is the growing need for private security, both personal
and for property. These private guards have become plentiful, and they have succumbed to corporate consolidation
where standards of conduct, pay, training, and other factors

can be regularized. The other path to legitimacy came in the form of services supplied to the U.S. military and other parts of the government.

The opportunity came when the U.S. military decided to embark on a path of transformation to achieve higher levels of flexibility and capability. To improve the quality of its forces despite an inability to compete with the private market for employment, the U.S. Department of Defense chose to outsource large portions of its functional needs to private contractors. These contractors supply everything from laundry and catering services for soldiers in the field to repair and maintenance of weapons systems to the security of military bases and personal security to diplomats. The men freed up from these activities have now been allocated to war-fighting duties.

The result of this shift, which mostly occurred during the drawdowns in the 1990s, can be seen in the U.S. force posture in Iraq. Some 100,000 civilians now support the 130,000 U.S. troops in the country. While this has set alarm bells off in the minds of nation-state patriots yearning for the bad old days, many are embracing this shift with open arms—despite signs of significant contractual abuse by many of the participants.

The reason is that these private military forces offer a level of flexibility and promise of efficiency when coping with threats to global market function. An example of this was seen most recently in the havoc created by Hurricane Katrina in New Orleans. When the federal government, because of bad management and legal barriers using federal forces, failed to act, PMCs stepped into some of the breaches. Companies such as Blackwater and others quickly sent forces to New Orleans to protect high-value property for corporate clients (from looters) and provided extraction details for high-net-worth individuals and valuable corporate employees.

PMCs weren't the only companies to respond quickly. Wal-Mart was quick to provide water and other essentials to the area, leveraging its vast supply system. The lesson was clear: these corporate participants, operating in a decentralized fashion, could provide a faster and more efficient response to a situation that was once only the province of government. In fact, the success of these corporate efforts was mostly limited by local and federal government interference. We can expect to see the use of PMCs continue to grow. For every local or global failure of nation-states to address critical problems, corporate participants in general and PMCs in particular will continue to gain ground. It's inevitable.

Transnational Gangs

On March 15, 2005, the Federal Bureau of Investigation took the War on Terrorism to one of the most violent and widespread gangs in the United States. One hundred members of Mara Salvatrucha (MS-13) were arrested in a nationwide dragnet—a small portion of the gang's estimated 8,000 to 10,000 members dispersed over thirty-one U.S. states. Most of those captured have been detained, arraigned, and deported to El Salvador or Honduras. Once back in Central America, where many haven't been for the majority of their lives, they join tens of thousands of other gang members undermining the viability of the Honduran and El Salvadoran states. This gang began on the streets of Los Angeles and has been exported to Central America.

Gangs Grow Up

The MS-13 isn't your ordinary gang. It is, according to Max Manwaring (of the Strategic Studies Institute), an example of a new breed of gang, what has been termed a *third-generation gang* (we could call it a global guerrilla).

In his paper "Street Gangs: The New Urban Insurgency," Manwaring provides a generational framework for understanding the evolution of gangs:

- First generation. Turf protection; unsophisticated leadership; opportunistic petty crime.
- Second generation. Organized for business and financial gain; broader geographical footprint; violence is slaved to the intimidation of commercial competitors and government interference.
- Third generation. Multinational footprint; extremely sophisticated transnational criminal operations (lawyers, banks, and so forth); political control of under-governed and/or underserved areas within target states; extreme interference in state function, including overt attempts at state control.

Third-generation gangs have ridden the rapid growth of the transnational criminal economy, which already has a UN-estimated gross world product of $2.5 trillion a year (this criminal economy grows in parallel with globalization). They are heavily involved in drugs, kidnapping, protection rackets, and smuggling of all types. To protect their activities, these gangs target governments with bribery and intimidation. Given that most of their activities are beyond the reach of any one government to influence, they have become very effective at subverting states through elimination of the state's monopoly on violence and the distortion of legitimate market activity.

Transnational Gangs as Global Guerrillas

Unlike historical guerrilla insurgencies, gangs don't want to run the state directly, don't have a central ideology or a comprehensive political program, and don't represent, protect, or enrich anybody but their members. Their main goal is to secure their existence and their right to unfettered activities by targeting states.

Third-generation gangs fit the model of global guerrillas perfectly. They operate, coordinate, and expand globally. They communicate worldwide without state restriction, often via the Internet. They engage in transnational crime. They participate in fourth-generation warfare, and their activities disrupt national and international systems. Finally, they coerce, replace, or fail states that stand in their way. In all these categories, they parallel the development of al-Qaeda and other terrorist organizations. Like al-Qaeda, these gangs are rivals of nation-states. Their organic growth has already pushed them into direct confrontation with states. In the future, we can expect to see:

- Gangs adopt systems sabotage to more easily coerce or fail recalcitrant states. The ability of gangs to buy expertise will ensure substantial access to the systems needed.
- Coordination between global guerrilla groups will develop to share weapons, expand criminal activities, and so on. The destruction of the state system is a powerful unifying force.
- Homegrown third-generation gangs will challenge the United States for control. From the Aryan Brotherhood to the MS-13, the United States is teeming with increasingly powerful gangs.

One thing that these hundreds, growing to thousands, of global guerrilla groups have in common is an affinity for systems disruption. To really understand how this can and will be used to fight and win against nation-states, let's dive into how it works.

5

SYSTEMS DISRUPTION

In January 2006, several men blew up two collocated pipelines in a mountain pass in southern Russia. These pipelines carried natural gas to the country of Georgia and were part of the Gazprom pipeline network. The work took only a couple of hours because the pipelines, both the primary and the backup system, were merely separated by a small river. Nearly simultaneously, another team attacked a power transmission pylon carrying high-voltage electricity to Georgia from Russia. The combination of the two attacks cut the entire country of Georgia off from both natural gas and electricity.

With only twenty-four hours' worth of natural gas reserves, the Georgian government flew into a panic. The country was in the middle of a severe cold snap, and without heat or light there was an immediate risk that some of the country's most vulnerable residents would perish. Quick community action mitigated much of this peril. Despite tremendous pressure from the government on the Russian suppliers, repairs took over a week to accomplish. During that entire week, Georgia was essentially operating at a preindustrial level.

The most disturbing aspect of the rise of global guerrillas is that they have found a way to fight nation-states strategically without the use of weapons of mass destruction. This method, collectively called *systems disruption,* uses sabotage of critical systems to inflict economic costs on the target state.

While sabotage has been with us forever as a form of warfare, it has only recently found an environment where it can take center stage. We are now living in a world where networks are at the center of our existence. They provide us with everything we need to live, from the moment the alarm clock wakes us in the morning until we turn out the light at night. Without these networks working around the clock, we generally feel as if we have lost some part of ourselves (at least I do when I can't access the Internet, watch TV, get a glass of water from the tap, or turn on a light).

The good news is that the efficient disruption of networks isn't as easy as just blowing things up randomly. Our networks are relatively good at dealing with random damage (they were designed for this because that type of damage occurs frequently due to storms or construction backhoes). To do it well, you have to understand the science of networks, which implies a barrier to entry. The bad news is that once you learn the science of networks, either through academic study or through trial and error, you can collapse networks relatively easily by merely hitting the right spot.

THE SYSTEMPUNKT

I call the right spot the *systempunkt.* It is a variation on a German term from blitzkrieg warfare. In blitzkrieg (remember Heinz Guderian's tanks rushing across northern France?), the point of greatest emphasis is called a *schwerpunkt*. It is the point, often identified by lower-level commanders, where the enemy front lines may be pierced by an explosive combination of multiple weapons systems (tanks, artillery, airpower, and so forth). Once the line is pierced, armored forces can drive deep into enemy territory to disrupt command, control, and logistics systems. When these systems are disrupted, the top-heavy military units they support collapse in confusion.

To global guerrillas, the point of greatest emphasis is the systempunkt. It is the point in a system (either an infrastructure system or a marketplace), usually identified by one of the many autonomous groups operating in the field, that will collapse the target system if it is destroyed. Within an infrastructure system, this collapse takes the form of disrupted flows that result in financial loss or supply shortages. Within a market, the result is a destabilization of the psychology of the marketplace that will introduce severe inefficiencies and chaos.

Our problem is that the global guerrillas we see in the long tail of this global insurgency are quickly learning how to detect and attack systempunkts.

THE ECONOMIC IMPACT OF ATTACKING SYSTEMPUNKTS

On August 14, 2003, between a few power lines sagging into trees and some incorrectly entered monitoring data, the total level of electrical power dipped in part of Ohio. Because of a few human and system failures, a cascade of power surges and generators going off-line spread across more than a hundred generators and most of the northeast, including Canada. What started as a minor fluctuation in the Ohio grid became a blackout affecting nearly fifty million people.

Immediately after the lights went out, there was speculation that it had been a terrorist attack. While it wasn't, it could have been. To really get a sense of how dangerous this is, let's examine what an attack on the power grid of the northeastern United States might look like. Andersen Consulting did a relatively thorough study of the impact ("Northeast Blackout to Reduce U.S. Earning $6.4 Billion"). Here are the highlights:

Economic Effect	Cost
Lost income and corporate profit	$3.12 to $5.12 billion
Spoilage (food and so forth)	$380 to $940 million
Additional police and emergency services	$15 to $100 million
Higher utility rates (to cover costs)	$1 to $2 billion
Total economic impact	$4.51 to $8.24 billion

As you can see from this analysis, the costs are staggering. It is even more sobering when you consider what it would take to generate this type of attack.

The attacks on 9/11 generated at least an order of magnitude more damage (both direct and indirect) than the Northeast power blackout—approximately $80 billion. Almost all the costs inflicted on 9/11 were incidental to the main objective of the attack, which was the destruction of American symbols recognizable the world over. To carry out that attack, a large network of participants (seventy to eighty, including the support networks) was assembled, and years of planning, training, and preparation were undertaken. We couldn't expect an attack of this magnitude to happen any more often than once every four to five years. Furthermore, given the current security environment, it is unlikely that a group that large would be able to plan an attack on this scale.

In contrast, an attack that replicated the *effects* of the Northeast power blackout would require a three- to five-man team. The preparation would require a few days doing network analysis and receiving light training on how to attack the target. The tools used for the attack could be as simple as a wrench or a propane tank (for explosive effect). Additionally, given the way these targets could be attacked, it is unlikely that any of the attackers would be caught, leaving them to attack again.

In stark contrast to the attack on 9/11, assaults on infrastructure systempunkts could occur once every couple of days. Furthermore, there is a plethora of systems that can be attacked, with a huge number of critical vulnerabilities. Put into perspective, this means that the *economic effects* of a comparable 9/11-level attack could be replicated by one small team attack once a month. If multiple teams were used, this could drop to one every week or less.

This exercise in logic isn't idle speculation. It is being put into practice across the world at an increasing level of frequency. Meanwhile, we continue to allocate our security resources as if this kind of attack will never happen here.

THE RETURNS ON INVESTMENT OF SYSTEMS DISRUPTION

The cost-benefit ratio is against us! Our cost is billions against the terrorists' cost of millions.

—Donald Rumsfeld[1]

When a system collapses, it amplifies the damage of the attack and provides rates of return up to a million times the initial investment (the cost of the attack). Within the structure of economic analysis, this means that the investment made in an attack can yield returns on investment (ROIs) equal to a million times the costs.

We saw this to a small extent on 9/11. For that event, the costs of the attack have been estimated to be as high as $500,000. The return, in terms of economic damage for the attack, has been estimated to be $80 billion. That is an ROI of sixteen thousand times the original investment. This seriously understates the case, however. Once the opportunity costs of the time taken to plan and carry out the attack as well as the loss of dozens of personnel, because of suicide and capture, are included in the calculation, the ROI is much, much less.

In contrast, systems disruption, such as what we have seen in Iraq, Nigeria, Pakistan, Russia, Georgia, and Thailand, offers much higher rates of return. Not only were these attacks much easier to plan but also they often didn't even cost the attackers their lives. The following are a couple examples from recent events.

In the summer of 2004, Iraq's global guerrillas attacked a southern section of the Iraqi oil pipeline infrastructure (Iraq has over 4,300 miles of pipelines). This attack cost the attackers an estimated $2,000 to produce. None of the attackers was caught. The effects of this attack were over $500 million in lost oil exports. The rate of return: 250,000 times the cost of the attack.

In February 2006, Nigerian guerrillas of the amorphous Movement for the Emancipation of the Niger Delta attacked the loading dock on Shell Oil's Forcados export platform. The attackers escaped without being captured or suffering casualties. The estimated cost of the attack was $2,000 (twenty men at a generous $100 each for the day). The cost to Shell was $400,000 in lost oil exports for an estimated two weeks and the indefinite shutdown of an adjacent oil field. The estimated lost revenue to Shell was over $50 million. The rate of return: 25,000 times the cost of the attack.

As you can see, the rates of return on these attacks are phenomenal. Even more important is that these attacks were easy to plan and carry out. Because the attackers weren't caught (nor have they been in almost all the attacks recorded since the turn of the twenty-first century), the organizations carrying out these attacks can repeat the effort in a sustainable way.

Cascades of Failure

There are two ways to disrupt networks. The obvious way is to pick a high-value facility and damage it. Despite the media's obsession with the supposed vulnerability of the United States' nuclear power facilities, this is typically tough to do. Facilities like these are often heavily guarded. The costs of an attack would likely be prohibitive and the rates of success low. A February 2006 attack by al-Qaeda on a major oil-processing facility in Saudi Arabia demonstrates the perils of this approach: the attackers didn't even get through the second layer of security despite considerable planning and triple car bombs. A more refined approach that yields better results is to use the dynamics of the network against itself, and this is exactly what we are seeing more and more.

The secret sauce of this approach is the cascade of failure. A cascade is similar to what you see when you line up a row of dominoes standing on their ends. If you hit the one at the front of the line, all the dominoes subsequently crash into one another and end up flat on the table. Infrastructure cascades operate in a similar fashion.

In general, cascade failures follow a simple process and can occur naturally because of random failures in complex systems. To demonstrate how this works, let's use as an example the disruption of an electrical grid because of a lightning storm.

First, a lightning strike causes a break in a line. Second, the demand for power this broken line services is shed to other lines, many of which are already near their capacity limits. These other lines are unable to handle the additional load and fail (to prevent damage to the lines). These initial failures shed demand to the remaining network. More overloaded lines fail, and so on. The end result is an avalanche of successive failures and a system-wide blackout.

Creating Cascades

Many of the systems we rely on have a unique vulnerability to cascading failures. They are called scale-free networks. For a more complete exploration of scale-free networks, I suggest you read Albert-Laszlo Barabasi's *Linked: How Everything Is Connected to Everything Else and What It Means for Business, Science, and Everyday Life*. Scale-free networks have two seemingly incompatible qualities. Barabasi studied networks where each node is free to link to any other. He discovered that these networks contain an unlimited number of links and that they counterintuitively also develop large, highly connected hubs.

The connectivity to these hubs is often described as *scale free*, in that there is no limit on how many different connections they have. Scale-free, hub-based networks are extremely robust to random failures. (Barabasi used the Internet in his original example, and you've surely discovered that losing your connection to the World Wide Web doesn't bring the whole thing down.) The hubs provide a high degree of cross-network connectivity that can prevent the disintegration of the network even if a large number of random failures occur. Given this robustness to random failures, it is easy to see why scale-free networks have become so common.

One commonly discussed example is the spread of sexually transmitted diseases (STDs). While every adult is (theoretically) free to link up with as many partners as possible, only a small number of people link up with a large number, becoming hubs. These high-volume partners are integral to the spread of STDs, such as the human immunodeficiency virus. If any one person drops out of the network, he or she won't shut down the network or slow the spread of STDs. If one of the high-volume nodes drops out of the network, however, it could significantly reduce the spread of STDs.

While scale-free networks are not made vulnerable by the loss of random nodes, however, they are extremely vulnerable to *intentional* disruption. If attackers can disrupt the operation of the hubs of a scale-free infrastructure network, the entire network can collapse in a cascade of failure. Another factor that makes networks vulnerable to cascades is tight coupling. Modern networks are often tightly interconnected to provide high levels of performance. This means that changes in one section of the network can cause rapid changes in another. This is a positive feature during normal usage, but when an intentional attack occurs, a tightly coupled network can propagate the disruption faster than what human operators can compensate for.

The final factor influencing cascades of failure is heterogeneity. This is a way of saying that the nodes of the network (the connection points) are different from one another. Within an electrical system, this means that some lines or substations have the capacity to handle high loads and (most) others can handle only low loads. Naturally, because most of our networks handle dynamic flows, in that electricity, fuel, or water travel through them to end users, the loss of high-capacity nodes can overwhelm the low-capacity nodes.

A good example of this is the interstate highway system where it passes through a major urban area. An overturned tractor-trailer on a high-volume highway brings traffic to a halt, and what is the result? There are backups on every other road, from tiny side streets to major multi-lane thoroughfares, as they try, and fail, to absorb the dispersed capacity.

The interplay of the scale-free dynamics, tight coupling, and heterogeneity that is present in almost all our infrastructure networks makes it relatively easy for a knowledgeable attacker to cause systemwide cascades of failure.

Interdependence

Besides cascades of failure within a single network, there is also the possibility that cascades of failure can sweep across networks. In modern economies, most infrastructure networks are tightly interconnected. This means that the electricity network helps run the transportation network, the water network, and the fuel (oil and natural gas) network. In turn, the fuel network and the transportation network (needed for repairs) help keep the electricity network running. Global guerrillas have proven to be increasingly adept at using these interconnections to cause cross-network cascades of failure.

For example, in the winter of 2005, Iraqi global guerrillas used their ability to disrupt power production to disrupt Iraq's oil exports. Guerrillas attacked oil and gas deliveries to a major power plant. Unable to operate, the power plant was forced to shut down. In turn, the electrical pumping stations at the southern oil terminal at Basra shut down for twenty-four hours because they couldn't get power. The cost? An estimated $100 million in lost oil exports.

In January 2006, Baloch guerrillas operating in western Pakistan shut down water pipelines feeding a natural gas processing plant. Water is used in the processing of the gas. Because of this shutdown, the plant was closed for a week.

THE VULNERABILITY OF U.S. NETWORKS TO DISRUPTION

Here's some deep analysis for those who really want to dive into this topic. In the paper "Structural Vulnerability of the North American Power Grid," Reka Albert, Istvan Albert, and Gary L. Nakarado analyze the vulnerability of the U.S. power grid to modern techniques of disruption. The key to this analysis is to find and disrupt network nodes that serve as hubs. They found the following:

- Highly connected nodes are a mix. Power engineering principles correctly suggest that the majority of highly connected nodes will be power plants. Contrary to expectations, however, a small number of transmission substation nodes are also highly connected.
- One percent (a total of fifty) of the transmission substations are high-load nodes. These high-load substations are nodes with high betweenness (a high number of shortest paths between nodes on the network). These substations are a combination of highly connected nodes and high-load throughput for long-haul connectivity (a critical part of the U.S. power grid since 50 percent of the electricity generated is allocated via the wholesale market, much of it over long distances because of not-in-my-backyard restrictions on local power production).
- Nine hundred of the distribution substations can potentially become isolated clusters (41 percent of the total). This means that these substations are only lightly connected to the grid. If the transmission sub-

station that connects them is taken off line because of an attack, they are disconnected from power generation and go dark.

The result of this analysis indicates that a cascading system failure can shut down 60 percent of the grid with the removal of only 2 percent of the high-load nodes. If only 1 percent is attacked, up to 40 percent of the grid goes dark.

Target: U.S. Oil System

Oil infrastructure vulnerability in the United States isn't limited to international production and transport because there are significant vulnerabilities within U.S. borders. As with most U.S. infrastructure, there are extreme levels of concentration because of underinvestment and efficiency. Allegro Energy Group's December 2001 report "How Pipelines Make the U.S. Energy System Work" provides insight into this issue:

- Transport concentration. A large majority of U.S. oil (68 percent) is delivered by domestic pipelines. The U.S. oil pipeline infrastructure is extremely concentrated with relatively few large pipelines. Additionally, U.S. pipelines ship more than just oil. They also provide transport for diesel and gas. An attack on a pipeline will affect multiple markets. Experience in Iraq shows that even limited physical attacks against oil pipeline infrastructure can disrupt transport for extended periods (months). These physical attacks can be made with relative ease.
- Control system concentration. As with the power system, the U.S. oil infrastructure relies on a security-free command and control system (a supervisory control and data acquisition network). This system

lacks encryption, operates on open networks, and is easily hacked (see my article "Power Peril" for more on control system vulnerabilities).

- Production concentration. The Gulf Coast provides 55 percent of domestic crude and 47 percent of refined product production. This presents a similar vulnerability to the Al Baqra oil terminal. A single, well-planned attack could provide strategic impact that could not be easily replaced.

How to Control the Golden Goose without Killing It

The ongoing campaign of infrastructure disruption in Iraq (oil, gas, electricity, water, and so forth) brings up an important question on strategy: Will global guerrillas strive for a complete shutdown of Iraq's infrastructure, or do they achieve more through a partial shutdown?

Lawrence of Arabia provides some insight into this. Lawrence's guerrilla campaign (for more on this read the fantastic book on Lawrence's strategy by B. H. Liddell Hart) against the Ottoman Turks was focused on the disruption of the Turkish rail system. However, his approach did not seek the total collapse of the rail system. In Lawrence's view, it was more important to control the rate of flow on the rail system than to shut it down entirely. If he had shut down the rail system, the Turkish troops who depended on it for supplies would have been withdrawn (and would have been used to reinforce the front against the British in Sinai and Palestine). In contrast, by restricting the flow on the system, the Turkish troops remained in place but didn't have the resources to do anything but stay in their garrisons. In essence, Lawrence used disruption to produce two desired effects (for more on this, read David A. Deptula's "Effects-Based Operations: Change in the

Nature of Warfare"): the paralysis of a large segment of the Turkish army and complete freedom of movement in 99 percent of Arabia.

A similar logic applies to the systems disruption operations in motion in Iraq today. Attacks by Iraq's global guerrillas keep Iraq's infrastructure below what is needed to adequately provide for the population. Additionally, there appears to be evidence that these attacks have moved into maintenance mode—just enough disruption to maintain current levels of insufficient output even though complete collapse is within their means. This makes sense if the desired effects are an extremely weak Iraqi state and the withdrawal of a chastened United States. Here's why partial disruption makes this possible:

- Complete collapse would create total war (via a bloody civil war). A complete urban or country takedown would prompt the state to launch a total war. This is a type of warfare that global guerrillas are not prepared or able to fight (in contrast, states are well suited to this). By keeping the level of damage below what would be considered fatal to the state, total war is avoided.

- Partial disruption delegitimizes the state (and the U.S. occupation). Partial paralysis creates a situation where the government is responsible for failures. Guerrilla attacks are lumped in with failures in system management and blamed on the state. This decrease in state legitimacy increases the need for people to depend on primary loyalties rather than on the state for solutions. Fragmentation equals good.

- Partial disruption maximizes economic attrition and provides the illusion that the situation is manageable. As a result, both Iraq and the United States continue to fight this war on the margins of a peace-time financial agenda. This peacetime budget is expensive, however, and the Iraqi state is unable to pay for these programs—disruption has stalled growth in both export and tax revenues. Additionally, the current situation continues to spur the United States to pour funds it can't afford into reconstruction (complete failure would likely halt inflows).

URBAN TAKEDOWNS

A rapid increase in urbanization and the proliferation of megacities have been salient trends of global economic development since World War II. These trends will be exploited in this war. Cities are both the center of gravity of modern urban economies and extremely vulnerable to global guerrilla systems sabotage—the leveraged infrastructure that cities rely on is the perfect target.

It is therefore important to understand what provides cities their cohesion and why they collapse. In a departure from fourth-generation warfare theory, this cohesion isn't provided by moral factors but by economic factors. A good source of insight into the economic factors that hold cities together is a post-9/11 report by James Harrigan and Philippe Martin of the Federal Reserve Bank of New York. Their analysis indicates the following:

- Cities form when aggregation is economically advantageous to both firms and workers.
- A city's size (its population of both firms and workers) is maintained through a market equilibrium, where the benefits of aggregation are balanced with the costs.
- Ongoing insults to this equilibrium, in the form of a terrorist tax, can cause a city to decline (disaggregate). This decline is defined as a transition to a new stable market equilibrium at a smaller size.

One way to look at terrorism's effect on cities is in the form of a tax. A terrorism tax is an accumulation of excess costs inflicted on a city's stakeholders by acts of terrorism. These include direct costs inflicted on the city by terrorists (systems sabotage) and indirect costs because of the security, insurance, and policy changes needed to protect against attacks. A terrorism tax above a certain level will force the city to transition to a lower market equilibrium (read: shrink). So, what is that level? Here's what Harrigan and Martin conclude:

- Singular terrorist events (black swans), such as 9/11, do not affect city viability. The costs of a singular event dissipate quickly. In contrast, frequent attacks (even small ones) on a specific city can create a terrorism tax of a level necessary to shift equilibriums.
- In the labor-pooling model of city formation, a terrorism tax of 7 percent will cause a city to collapse to a lower equilibrium. Labor-pooling equilibrium reflects the benefits of aggregating workers in a single location. Workers get higher wages and more choices, while firms can stabilize wages (no one firm can deplete the market) and more candidates.
- In the core-periphery model of city formation, a terrorism tax of 6.3 percent will push a city to a lower equilibrium. The core-periphery model is based on transportation costs. Firms generate transportation savings by concentrating in a single location next to suppliers and customers. Customers and workers glean the benefit of lower transportation costs by locating near jobs and goods.

The models used here are likely insufficient to fully explain why a city is in equilibrium. However, it is a good approximation. As a rule of thumb, a terrorism tax of 10 percent would be sufficient to push a city to significantly lower equilibriums—it would cause workers and firms to leave the city for other locations until the city ceased to be a target or became less expensive to defend.

If we apply this model to New York City, the terrorism tax necessary to collapse the city would be $40 billion a year (10 percent of New York City's annual economy of $400 billion a year). London would be $23 billion ($236 billion), Paris would be $13 billion ($131 billion), and so forth. As large as these numbers are, it isn't hard to see how quickly they can mount. For example, the Northeast blackout in August 2003 indicates that the power loss to New York City cost approximately $1 billion a day. So would forty days without power push New York City down to a lower economic potential level?

THE AMORPHOUS THREAT

The nearly unlimited power that infrastructure disruption provides nonstate groups isn't even the most alarming aspect about the new way of war. These groups have developed a new method of organization that leverages the power of global communications networks, provides rapid innovation, and protects them against nation-state counterpressure.

This new way of organizing means no one has been able to develop a strategy for containment or victory over them. You can't kill their leaders, because they don't need them. You can't reliably prevent further attacks, because they're small scale, dispersed, and unpredictable. You can't outmaneuver or outsmart them, because their innovative organization system makes that nearly impossible. Welcome to the open-source war.

6

OPEN-SOURCE WARFARE

In the 1966 movie *The Battle of Algiers* (which was once required viewing for senior U.S. officers going to Iraq), the French commander running the counterterrorist operation gives a briefing to his commanders. He has been given a mandate to destroy the insurgency in Algeria. In the briefing, he describes how insurgencies are organized, based on his hard-won experience in the resistance to German occupation. He starts with a cell composed of three to five people. These people are the decision-making body. Two people in the decision-making body in turn recruit an additional two people to build two more cells. The two new recruits don't know each other, nor do they know anyone above them except the person who recruited them. These new cells then form two more cells each, ad infinitum.

To destroy this insurgency, according to the French commander, you have to turn one of the people in the lower-level cells and work your way up to the top. He does this methodically throughout the movie, cell by cell, using torture as a means to grease the skids. Eventually, he kills the top cell leaders. This movie accurately captures the timeworn process of unraveling a hierarchically managed, ideologically driven insurgency. Unfortunately, it doesn't work in today's environment.

My question is this: What if warfare was reinvented and nobody bothered to tell the Pentagon?

THE TERRORIST IS DEAD, LONG LIVE THE TERRORIST

On June 7, 2006, the U.S. military in Iraq carried out a successful operation it had long been hoping for. Thanks to Jordanian intelligence, drawn from Abu Musab al-Zarqawi's most recent public videotape, the U.S. military discovered the location of his safe house near Ba'quba. Minutes after an F-16 dropped two 500-pound bombs on the house, coalition forces arrived on the scene to find him mortally wounded and gasping for air. Within moments he was dead.

As many smart commentators of every stripe have pointed out, this was excellent news but would do little to stop the insurgency in Iraq.

Al-Zarqawi was best categorized as a violence capitalist, very similar to Osama bin Laden, who supported and incubated guerrilla entrepreneurs of the new open-source warfare model. In this role, he was an instigator of violence and not the leader of a vast hierarchical insurgency.

In the early phases of the guerrilla war in Iraq, al-Zarqawi was operational as the commander of a small cell. His group was able, through early large-scale attacks, to set a plausible promise (an idea that many other groups could rally around) for the Iraqi insurgency. Namely, that it was possible to successfully fight the U.S. occupation.

During late 2004 and early 2005, his operational value diminished as the number of groups that were engaged in the war proliferated. During that time, he was focused on expanding the target set of the insurgency to include infrastructure, corporations, and Iraqi military units. Later in 2005, his operational activities were focused on shifting the plausible promise of the insurgency from ousting the Americans to fighting Shiite domination (sectarian war) through attacks on Shiite civilians and symbols.

By early 2006, al-Zarqawi's operational activities were all but over. He had succeeded in seeding the original insurgency and shifting the plausible promise to include sectarian warfare. During this final phase, al-Zarqawi moved into a role of strategic communicator, much like bin Laden's role today. In this role, he produced videos that were distributed to a global audience through the Internet and global media.

Shortly after al-Zarqawi's death, Sheikh Abu Hamza al-Muhajer apparently stepped into his role and rose high on the coalition's most wanted list.

Has the insurgency really developed a kind of war where killing its leaders doesn't hurt it?

AN OPEN APPROACH

Our differences were based on some principles, but even those were just for a temporary phase. We are fighting a common enemy.

—Gul Mohammad, a commander of a guerrilla faction in Afghanistan[1]

The Iraqi insurgent movement is made up of at least seventy different groups. New groups seem to emerge almost every week. As far as we can tell, there isn't any identifiable command and control structure for the movement. Al-Qaeda in Iraq, for all the press it receives, is only a small percentage (some estimate only 5 percent) of the entire insurgency. The long tail of insurgent participants in Iraq examined in chapter 4 doesn't fully explain how the insurgency continues to gain ground against U.S. forces.

The most likely explanation is the simplest. It has become an open-source insurgency. Open source is a method of software development that has emerged over the last decade. In traditional corporate software development, the process is extremely structured and tightly controlled. This is particularly true for the source code—the core nuts and bolts of the program or system. It is usually accessible to only key individuals or teams because of economic, legal, and control issues.

In contrast, the open-source model makes all the code (both the source code and everything built on top of it) available without meaningful restriction. Anyone can read it. Additionally, anyone who wants to is allowed to work on it.

It's easy to see that an immediate benefit of this approach is that it enables a potentially vast pool of programmers to modify the code, fix it, and extend it at will. Furthermore, because this is a labor of love and not one for money, the direct costs of this approach are nearly nil (participants have to find their own ways to fund their efforts).

There are, however, several potential downsides to open-source development. The project needs to be interesting enough to attract participants. If it is only interesting to a few people, then it won't take off. This problem can't be routed around, so it is a hard requirement.

A second problem has to do with organizational focus. The interesting work-around for this is that the open-source approach uses a community model. The community joins together based on a common premise: the promise of the software. Based on their abilities, individuals provide both what the community needs done and what they individually think would add to the project.

Most people who know what it's like to work in corporate hierarchies can't imagine that a system like this would produce anything of interest. They are wrong. It works extremely well. Despite its lack of organizational discipline, open-source software development has been used to develop amazingly complex and useful programs, from Linux to the Apache server (the dominant Web server on the Internet). Hordes of programmers have joined communities built around these projects to contribute to their success. The weight of the brainpower contributed by these volunteers is far in excess of that possible by any one company or group of companies. The resolution of conflict (on goals or modifications) between these disparate volunteers is simple: *Will the community accept it as an improvement?*

By now, most readers are familiar with Wikipedia, the open-source encyclopedia. It has been compiled, edited, and updated by its users, which at times seems to include everyone with a connection to the Internet. Most users put only a tiny amount of effort into it, in their area of expertise, because they simply can't stand to see the entry they've come across continue to be incomplete, incorrect, or disorganized. Despite lacking the budget or expertise of, say, the *Encyclopaedia Britannica,* Wikipedia covers an astonishing number of topics—far more than a traditional encyclopedia. (That's because, with unlimited space and simplicity of use, it's also become the long-tail encyclopedia.) While many have complained that it is not quite error free, the more popular the article, the less likely it is to contain errors. The more eyes on that page, the fewer the bugs. It may also not have the level of depth *Britannica* has on major topics, but it is amazingly deep on current events and pop culture. If something happened an hour ago, it's probably already been updated on Wikipedia. With any mass open-source project, such as Wikipedia, being the aggregate of so much combined intelligence, it may not be perfect, but there will never be anything more broad-based and quick.

THE PLAUSIBLE PROMISE

Iraq's global guerrillas, and increasingly al-Qaeda (although some of their attacks in 2005 and early 2006 show that they are still slightly more centrally directed than their brethren), have adopted open-source warfare (OSW). An OSW effort starts with a plausible promise, an idea that if we all work together this effort can produce amazing results. In software, this is often an early alpha version of the system that actually does something interesting. In warfare, this is an attack (like 9/11 or some of the early bombings in Iraq) that excites the imagination of potential participants.

This promise is the central connection between all the members in the community. Each member can have specific motivations that are substantially different from any of the others. In the case of warfare, these alternative motivations can be patriotism, hatred of occupation, ethnic bigotry, religious fervor, tribal loyalty, or what have you. It doesn't matter as long as they agree with the plausible promise.

HACKING WARFARE

In OSW, the source code of warfare is available for anyone who is interested in both modifying and extending it. This means the tactics, weapons, strategies, target selection, planning methods, and team dynamics are all open to community improvement. Global guerrillas can hack at the source code of warfare to their hearts' delight. The only caveat is that any changes need to be perceived as valuable to the advancement of the plausible promise. Here's a shorthand to the philosophy of hacking warfare I've created by adapting Eric S. Raymond's rules from "The Cathedral and the Bazaar"[2] to warfare:

- **Release (software updates) early and often.** Don't wait for a perfect plan. In war, this means try new forms of attacks against different types of targets as soon and as often as possible.
- **Given a large enough group of codevelopers, any problem will be seen as obvious and solved by someone.** Linus Torvald, the coordinator behind Linux—one of the most successful open-source software projects—coined a law: "Given enough eyeballs, all [software] bugs are shallow." If enough insurgents attempt to attack a target using different tactics, eventually some participant will find a way to succeed.
- **Your codevelopers (beta testers) are your most valuable resource.** The other guerrilla networks in the bazaar make for valuable allies. They will innovate on your original plans, swarm on identified weaknesses, and create protective system noise.
- **Recognize good ideas from your codevelopers.** Simple attacks that have an immediate and far-reaching impact should be adopted.
- **Perfection is achieved when there is nothing left to take away (simplicity).** The easier the attack is, the more easily it will be adopted. Complexity prevents swarming that both amplifies and protects.
- **Tools are often used in unexpected ways.** An attack method can often be reused in unexpected ways.

THE BAZAAR

A great description of the dynamics of OSW is a bazaar. People are trading, haggling, copying, and sharing. To an outsider it can look chaotic. It's so different from the quiet intensity and strict order of the cathedral-like Pentagon. This dynamic may be why Arab groups were some of the first guerrilla movements to pick up on this new method and apply it to warfare.

According to the perspective of the organized military, the problem with a bazaar is that it lacks a center of gravity—a centralized command center that can be destroyed or a single set of motivations that can be undermined through psychological or political operations. It is virtually immune to these approaches.

Additionally, the OSW network is extremely flexible with low barriers to entry—to wit, new clusters of individuals coming and going as they please. They can even fork from the main group if their plausible promise changes as we saw recently with the departure of al-Qaeda and Ansar al-Sunna from the main Iraqi OSW network. Furthermore, the OSW network offers a way for groups to stay small and therefore under the radar of external state-based observers. The network compensates for the small size of the individual groups that participate.

Finally, OSW networks are extremely innovative. The bazaar atmosphere makes it easy for innovations to develop and percolate among the members. They don't need a single operational genius, just a large number of average members working together. This explains why new innovations in improvised explosive device (IED) technology develop so fast to overcome U.S. countermeasures. It also explains the rapid shift in focus of the insurgency. In one month, the focus is on attacks that target the U.S. military; the next, it is focused on systems disruption of Iraqi infrastructure. The insurgency has an incredible knack for finding the most vulnerable targets that offer the greatest returns.

The Bazaar's Economics

One interesting and unique aspect of OSW as we see it in practice in Iraq is that it has developed a robust and complex economy to both complement and extend its activities. This economy has three elements:

- **Investment.** New funding from global sources is pouring into Iraq's bazaar—it has become the "hot" place for the globally mobile capital of violence.
- **Outsourcing.** The bazaar is comfortable accepting and incorporating members that participate for financial gain. The complexity of the market for IEDs demonstrates this.
- **Crime.** Criminal enterprise is not only accepted, it is encouraged. For example, threats to gasoline suppliers in Baghdad both aid the insurgency and provide a lucrative means of revenue through the black market.

The bazaar's flexible approach to economic incentives will make the integration into transnational criminal networks (which exhibit many of the same properties of open-source development) extremely easy.

More important, when taken together this means it is extraordinarily difficult to guard against future attacks. Guerrillas will put every new defense to the test in myriad ways. Any attempt to prevent one attack will have no effect on the others. And if one security method is breached, it will be breached again and again by other groups that copy the method of attack and swarm on the target.

Lessons from Phishing Networks

Christopher Abad, a research scientist at Cloudmark (a spam-filtering company), has done some amazing analysis on the phishing marketplace.[3] Phishing is a method of identity theft that uses fake e-mails and bogus Web sites to entice unwary consumers to disclose financial information (account details, credit card numbers, or personal data). This information is captured and used in financial fraud. It is a big business.

To deconstruct a phishing network, Abad used an automated data collection system that monitored chat rooms and activity on compromised servers. He found that the network consisted of loosely affiliated groups with lots of horizontal specialization rather than vertically integrated gangs. He proposed the following structure for the phishing microeconomy:

- **Automated unregulated chat rooms.** This network, often controlled by bots (code that automates activities and allows remote management), provides the basis for the marketplace. It provides an efficient and secure method for discovering information and conducting transactions.
- **Mass e-mailers.** Individuals who specialize in sending large volumes of e-mail (sometimes through worm-enabled bot networks). These e-mails initiate contact with the consumer.
- **Template providers.** Design specialists who create the look and feel of financial institution e-mails and Web sites.
- **Server managers.** Individuals who can compromise Internet servers and operate them remotely without detection. These servers collect information from consumers.
- **Cashers.** Buyers of financial information who can use it to generate bogus ATM cards and other forms of financial fraud.

The twenty-first-century criminal economies like the phishing economy demonstrate the same degree of decentralized self-organization we see in the market for IED manufacture and deployment in Iraq. Both markets aren't controlled by even a collection of gangs. Instead, they consist of a large network of individuals, gangs, tribes, and clans that trade, sell, share, and collaborate to make money and sometimes create mayhem. Additionally, both networks exhibit strikingly high levels of:

- **Efficiency.** The costs for component services are low and very competitive. Financial information can cost as little as $0.50 a record. Emplacement of an IED can cost $50.
- **Innovation.** New methods of attack and new target sets are constantly being discovered. Both groups rapidly leverage open Internet information to refine their target set. For example, in the case of phishing, the security community's chatter provides insight into corporate vulnerabilities and exploits. Iraqi guerrillas use Google maps to plot ambushes and IED emplacement.
- **Resilience.** These networks are able to resist discovery and networkwide collapse. One major factor in their resilience is their ability to transcend national boundaries and leverage a lack of local organic control (street-level enforcement).

The arrival of these "black" networks will likely lead to the following:

- **Network wars.** These networks are not a single entity. They can go to war. For example, Russian bot farmers recently attacked (denial of service) Chechen

Web sites in retaliation for terrorist activity against Russian targets.

- **The emergence of generic networks.** Skill sets from one network type can transfer to the other. The same technologies and techniques used for phishing and other criminal networks can be used to improve the efficiency of terrorist networks and provide a means of self-funding. Generic networks that combine criminal enterprise and terrorist and guerrilla activity are growing. We see this in Iraq today with the fluid market for hostages.

- **Rapid growth.** As global connectivity increases, non-state networks in the developing world will grow faster than those in the developed world due to hierarchical restrictions. This new connectivity allows them to transcend transnational barriers to coordination and create areas of local chaos.

SWARMS

Another interesting aspect of OSW is how it attacks. The approach we have seen in Iraq is based on an old method called *swarming*.[4]

For hundreds of years, swarming tactics have been successfully used in wars by a variety of organizations, from the tribal Parthians (horse archers) to twentieth-century Germans (U-boats), and conventional armies have had mixed success defending against swarming foes. In his battle with swarming Parthians, Alexander the Great was able to use a portion of his forces as bait to attract them, and then catch them with the remainder of his forces in a hammer-and-anvil operation. George Custer, however, wasn't so lucky.

There are two types of swarming: massed and dispersed. A good example of a massed swarm is a (disturbed) hive of bees: they begin as a unit, then break apart and swarm on the target. By contrast, dispersed swarming is what the Revolutionary War Minutemen did to the British redcoats while they retreated from Concord. This is largely what we are seeing in Iraq today, and it is more difficult to defend against because the attacker never presents a massed target.

Historically, swarming is successful only when it scores high in elusiveness, long-range firepower (arrows, for example), and superior intelligence about the enemy (Iraq's and al-Qaeda's swarmers score high in all areas). Iraqi guerrillas don't attack a single target but rather a target of a single type. For example, a guerrilla group takes a civilian hostage who works for a Turkish trucking company. This hostage drama results in the trucking company's withdrawal from Iraq. In response, other guerrilla groups swarm on the same category of target. They take truckers from other companies hostage to force those companies to withdraw. These attacks take place across the entire country from Al-Fallujah to Baghdad to Mosul.

As we continue to fight this war, we can expect to see swarming expand to the larger realm, because global guerrillas now operate in dozens of countries. A target (including the global operations of a multinational company) could be swarmed from points all over the globe. This kind of operational and strategic threat by a dispersed swarm would be a first in the history of warfare.

COORDINATION

Besides direct face-to-face, cell phone, or Internet contact among insurgents in Iraq's OSW network, communication can also occur through a process called *stigmergy*.

Stigmergy is a term used in biology (by the French biologist Pierre-Paul Grasse) to describe environmental mechanisms for coordinating the work of independent actors (for example, ants use pheromones to create trails and people use blog links to establish information paths for others to follow). The term is derived from the Greek words *stigma* (sign) and *ergon* (to act). Stigmergy can be used as a mechanism to understand underlying patterns in swarming activity. As such, it can be applied to the understanding of swarming attacks by diverse bands of global guerrillas. The stigmergic information system that operates in Iraq is the bazaar of violence. A knowledge of stigmergy is a key to understanding how these groups learn.

Stigmergic systems use simple environmental signals to coordinate the actions of independent agents (each with their own decision-making process). These signals are used to coordinate scalable, robust, and dynamic activity. This activity is often much more intelligent than the actions capable by the individual actors (in this case, individual global guerrilla groups). There are four basic mechanisms of environmental coordination:

- **Marker based.** Markers or signs left by actors influence the action of other actors. In the global guerrilla context, this is the site of an attack and the news of the attack that is delivered by the media. The description of the attack in the media is the stigmergic marker for others to follow.
- **Sematectonic.** Environmental conditions influence the behavior of all actors in the system. For guerrillas, multiple attacks on a certain type of target can generate a security response by the nation-state that changes the potential of attacks against that type of target in the immediate future. An increased security presence for those types of targets is a sematectonic signal to select something else.
- **Quantitative.** The environmental signals are of a single scalable type. The size of a global guerrilla

attack on a given location can meter the scale of the security response.

- **Qualitative.** The environmental signals are of a varied type that change the message based on their combination. Different types of attacks on the same target (the length of power outages in Baghdad) will yield information on the type of attack that is the most effective.[5]

A deeper understanding of the stigmergic signaling between global guerrillas will enable the development of ways to disrupt their activity. These examples are by no means exhaustive.

EMERGENT INTELLIGENCE

One final mechanism we should examine is the potential that Iraq's OSW network may be exhibiting signs of emergent intelligence. It is possible that the interactions of the participants within these networks can yield a type of macrointelligence that allows it to tackle strategic goals. This form of intelligence is called *emergent intelligence*.

The term *emergence* describes a set of high-level characteristics or capacities that evolve unexpectedly from a complex system. Illustrative examples of emergence are the patterns that form when fish school or birds flock. Each fish or bird, following simple programming, combines to form a group that exhibits emergent characteristics.

Emergence isn't limited to simple visual patterns. It can also describe group intelligence without the benefit of a central command function. The idea for this came out of observations of insects and other complex social networks. Observers find that an ant colony or a beehive, despite the lack of any centralized control element, can respond to changes in environmental conditions (sources of food, threats, and so forth) on a group level. Further-more, the emergent intelligence of the group matures the longer it has been in existence. It becomes more complex, nuanced, and adaptive.

The same description of intelligence can be applied to a set of groups engaged in OSW. As we have seen in Iraq and other locations, the behavior of these insurgencies as a whole seems to learn, achieve goals, and engage in self-preservation, despite the vast differences in how individual groups are motivated.

The requirements for emergent intelligence are still in their infancy. However, a simple list has been formulated by Steven Johnson in his book on the topic, *Emergence: The Connected Lives of Ants, Brains, Cities, and Software*:[6]

- A critical mass of participation is necessary. A certain minimum number of participants, either individuals or component groups, are necessary for microaction to translate into macroaction. It also means that without a minimum number of interactions between these participants, the statistical nature of macrointelligence won't emerge. The simple catchphrase for this is *more is different.*

- A local focus is useful. The participants of the network need to be focused on local activity. The simplicity of their focus is a feature and not a bug because it prevents activity that may upset the entire organism's operation. The simple catchphrase is *local action, global impact.*

- Random interactions are necessary. The individual actors in the network must interact in a random way. These interactions provide fluidity to the network's learning process that produces unexpected variations at the macrolevel. A simple catchphrase is *do the unexpected.*

- Pattern matching is a necessity. Individual actors must be able to see patterns from local activities of their coworkers. These patterns form "signposts" or "maps" that lead them to refine their own actions. This is the stigmergy explored earlier. A simple catchphrase is *read the writing on the wall.*
- Openness to interaction. A willingness to interact with others is required. Without these interactions, no group intelligence can form. A simple catchphrase is *be promiscuous.*

Analysis of the various complex insurgent movements in places like Iraq, Nigeria, Russia, and Pakistan reveals that emergent intelligence is likely evolving. The complex interactions of local participants have yielded complex network behavior. The groups are constantly finding new target sets to exploit, new tactics for attacking these targets, and new forms of self-protection that go beyond the innovation of local participants. As a group, they are getting smarter.

This means we can't rely on our think tanks and strategy sessions to figure out a way out of this. We may have some individuals who are smarter, more educated, or better planners, but the collective intelligence of insurgent movements will still be good enough to match or best our collective intelligence.

A Guerrilla Oil Cartel?

We can't outsmart them, protect against them, or take out their leadership. How far can they take this?

As an example of what the combination of emergence of global guerrillas, systems disruption, and OSW means, let's take a hard look at the global oil market. Loosely organized global guerrillas can now, at will, curtail the

supply of oil through low-tech attacks (systems disruption) on facilities in Iraq, Saudi Arabia, Nigeria, and Central Asia (and it is only a matter of time before Mexico is
added to the list). The amount of oil already under the
effective control of these guerrillas exceeds 5 million barrels a day, more than Saudi Arabia's 2 million barrels a
day of swing production.

It's important to note that this capacity to disrupt production is substantially different from any terrorist threat
we have faced in the past. With terrorism, the potential
damage has always been due to a single large attack on a
major facility (extremely difficult to accomplish and relatively easy to compensate for). Today's threat is based on
sustainable disruption—ongoing, easy, low-tech attacks
that are nearly impossible to defend against (everything
from pipeline destruction to employee kidnapping). The
goals of these attackers can be divided into three comple-
mentary categories:

- **Delegitimization of the target state.** Attacks meant
  to "hollow out" the state by preventing the delivery
  of critical services or a denial of income and/or
  investment.
- **Coercion of core developed states.** To damage the
  United States and the developed world, in general,
  through economic means.
- **Criminal profit.** By increasing the prices of oil and
  its refined products, the profits generated by criminal enterprise (bunkering oil, smuggling, and so
  forth) are radically improved.

This situation is merely the first stage in the larger
long war between nonstate groups and nation-states. It is
by no means the worst of what we have to deal with.
Other, more profound developments will occur as this

trend progresses. In the meantime, given that the demand for oil continues to increase (because of the growth of India and China), combined with the inability to bring new supplies online, the price of oil may continue to climb to well over $100 a barrel as:

- The guerrilla oil cartel expands into new locations. The success of guerrillas to control production in Iraq and Nigeria will spawn similar developments in Russia, Central Asia, and Mexico.
- Market collusion. So far, there aren't many signs of coordination between guerrillas and global financial interests (hedge funds, wealthy individuals, current members of the Organization of the Petroleum Exporting Countries, and so forth). There will be. There is too much money to be made.

The hypothetical emergence of a guerrilla oil cartel points us in an interesting direction. What if the need of newly superempowered individuals to control their economic destiny combines with systems disruption and OSW? This combination provides the organizational structure, the means of warfare, and the economy (financial fuel)—all the elements needed to become a virtual state. In fact, this is exactly what we are seeing.

Part III

HOW GLOBALIZATION WILL PUT AN END TO GLOBALIZATION

7

GUERRILLA ENTREPRENEURS

On August 3, 2005, fifteen U.S. Marines set out in a massive armored amphibious vehicle to sweep the periphery of the western Iraqi town of Haditha. The town had been in the hands of elements of the guerrilla groups al-Qaeda and Ansar al-Sunna for months. These groups had leveraged the lack of any meaningful presence of U.S. and Iraqi troops to put the town under Islamic law. To reward the town, they intimidated the management of the local power plant at the adjacent Haditha dam on the Euphrates to supply the town with continuous electricity, an unheard-of luxury in Iraq at the time.

The sweep, as they often do, rapidly ran afoul of an improvised explosive device (IED). Typically, an armored vehicle of this size (despite the fact its armor was lighter than typical ground vehicles) would be impervious to an IED. Today was different, however. The open-source development system of Iraq's guerrillas had produced another innovation: a massive-focused charge bomb.

The IED explosion flipped the 31-ton troop carrier over onto its back and caused it to burst into flames.[1] Fourteen of the fifteen marines died due to either the explosion or the fire. One was seriously wounded.

If we dig deeper into what led up to the deaths of these marines, and hundreds like them across Iraq, we see something new in warfare: a modern marketplace driven by guerrilla entrepreneurs.

LAWRENCE OF ARABIA

The idea of an entrepreneur of violence isn't new. Its roots extend to the very dawn of warfare. This is particularly true in the Arab world. If we look at the twentieth century, a good example is Lawrence of Arabia's guerrilla war against the Turks in Arabia and Syria during World War I.

Lawrence landed in Arabia during World War I because of a strange confluence of events. His mission was to aid the Arab tribes in a revolt against the Turks, who were allied with Germany and Austria and who had ruled Arabia for years (coincidentally, Lawrence began his guerrilla operations just miles from where Osama bin Laden grew up).

Due to the influence of religious differences and the proximity of Islam's most holy locations, the British were unable to send regular troops to fight the war in Arabia. It was left to key individuals, entrepreneurs if you will, to accomplish. Lawrence, by happenstance and by talent, became such a person.

To assemble his army, Lawrence was faced with the feckless structure of Arabian tribes. While ethnic rivalry played a part in motivating the recruitment of his guerrillas, the only method that proved constant was the promise of loot. Guerrillas flowed into and out of his unit as they took their fill of loot from raids on trains and outposts. These Arab entrepreneurs, acting like most military men over the ages (except recently), saw war as a rewarding financial activity. The same is true today in the IED marketplace inside Iraq.

IRAQ'S IED MARKETPLACE

What will the future of war look like? When these trends take on more momentum, and spread farther across the globe, what will the long-term effects be? For one thing, the more attacks we see, the more attacks we will see. And each will be more innovative and effective than the last. Iraq's IED attacks, for example, have become more effective, more competitive, and more rewarding over time, not less, as most Americans sitting at home might expect. If the military has made a goal of trying to stop them, why would it be getting easier, which is what seems to be happening?

Copious evidence indicates that Iraq's guerrillas aren't organized in a hierarchical pattern. The initial organizational structures built by Saddam Hussein in his command bunker have long since mutated, under the withering gaze of the U.S. Army, into something else entirely. Instead, Iraq's guerrillas are constituted by a plethora of autonomous cells that operate independently.

As we see in a modern competitive marketplace with high-quality information flow, these granular guerrilla cells can combine and recombine to focus on specific American units (as well as contractors). To see how this works, let's get into the nuts and bolts. For an excellent description of this, we turn to the work of Greg Grant from the *Defense News*. His description of the structure of the IED marketplace in Iraq is based mainly on the information gained by the military from interrogations of captured guerrillas.

The organization and execution of most IED operations in Iraq is commercial. Very skilled IED cells, typically not more than six to eight people, often hire themselves out as a package. To market themselves, they even advertise on the Internet as *freelancers* (to use a term with mercenary roots) and are usually contracted on a temporary or per-job basis.

If we were to map the hierarchy of this operation, we would see the following:

- **The financier.** At the top of the typical organizational chart of an IED cell is the financier or planner from a well-known group. This "money man" supplies the financial resources for the operation and to the extent possible remains anonymous to most members of the cell.
- **The bomb maker.** The next level of the organization is the man who constructs the bomb. These bomb makers construct their weapons in a multitude of small "factories" scattered across Iraq. A bomb is often constructed on a just-in-time basis for an operation that has already been planned. If a car bomb is made (vehicle-borne IED), the car is first hollowed out in an assembly line–like process and modified in an auto chop shop. Extra suspension is added and the windows are blackened. The vehicle is then driven to other locations, where the bomb and other components are added.
- **The emplacer.** Because of the requirements of this job, the emplacer typically has some level of military expertise. He must move the IED to the target location without being noticed at great risk to himself. Typical payments for this service are as low as $50. Techniques used to place bombs range from deceptive "tire-changing operations" to roll bys (where the bomb is dropped through a hole in the floor of the car).

- **The triggerman.** This man sets the ambush for the U.S. convoy and lies in wait. He detonates the bomb with either a remote wireless device (for example, a garage door opener) or a wire connection.

The work of a fully staffed cell follows a methodical operations process that usually takes five days. During these days of preparation, time is spent conducting reconnaissance for target selection, pattern mapping of selected targets, and vulnerability analysis of specific vehicles. Cells have even used hoax IEDs in plain view to test the responses of targets.

This entrepreneurial culture isn't limited to tactical operations in Iraq. They extend to the geopolitical strategic level.

FIGHTING A THOUSAND TINY ARMIES

In the future, it will become harder and harder to put a name and a face to our enemies. Just as the attacks will be smaller and more numerous, so will the armies that carry them out against us.

The network organization of the team that attacked on 9/11, for example, provides us a great deal of insight into how networks work and what to expect in the future. To get insight into this, we need to turn to Valdis Krebs, a management consultant and organizational network expert. After doing some especially insightful analysis of the 9/11 attacks, he found that:

- **The attackers used a sparse operational network.** The nineteen members of the operational cells (the actual 9/11 hijackers) were isolated along a sparse network. The average number of hops between any two members of the network was a high 4.75. To mitigate this lack of connectivity, key members made connections to other key members in the network through brief face-to-face coordination meetings.

- **A larger administrative network supported the operational teams.** The administration network provided a means to "keep alive" many of the weak connections between sparsely connected members of the operational network.

- **A leadership structure existed despite a lack of formal hierarchy.** When the network is looked at in its entirety (operational plus administrative), Mohammed Atta emerges as the leader. Atta had twenty-two connections to other people in the network, much more than any other, which gave him control of the operation.

Despite this organic nature (al-Qaeda didn't "design" this network, it grew out of necessity), the design worked extremely well. Here are the dynamics:

- **The interplay of sparseness in operations and the closeness of the administrative support function enhance the workings of the network.** Because no one member knew a majority of the others, security was improved. Yet the administrative network mitigated the detrimental aspects of this configuration (less learning, poorer planning, and so forth).

- **Trust between members of the network was based on deep relationships.** Many of the relationships between members of the 9/11 terrorist network were developed years before in the al-Qaeda training camps in Afghanistan (today, shared educational experiences in the madrassas—Islamic schools of a

Saudi model—can serve to produce a similar level of social capital).

The 9/11 terrorist networks eventually served as the model for all of al-Qaeda. The following are some important lessons we can glean from this analysis:

- **Expect these networks to be run by relative unknowns.** Neither Osama bin Laden, nor any of his top aides, were directly involved in the network map. He does not micromanage, nor will most global guerrilla managers. This implies that senior leadership removal is not likely to have any measurable effect on ongoing global guerrilla operations.
- **Assassination of a single operational leader will not work.** Despite the concentration of leadership and unique skills in Atta, his assassination would not have prevented the operation. A second emergent leader with a high degree of connectivity was present: Marwan al-Shehhi. If Atta were removed, his loss would have eliminated one cell from the operational team (he was a pilot) while leaving most of the network intact.
- **Strategic attacks are possible with a network of less than seventy people.** The small size and low cost of the 9/11 operations should give pause to all counterterrorist planners. This means that normal estimates of opposition manpower may be of little use because the number of people necessary to plan and execute five 9/11s a year is less than four hundred people.

Now that we understand how the 9/11 network worked, how does this apply to the organizational structures we see in Iraq's insurgency and others across the world? The first lesson is that distributed, dynamic terrorist networks can't scale like hierarchical organizations. The same dynamics that make them resilient against attack put absolute limits on their size. If so, what are those limits?

A good starting point is to look at the limits of group size within peaceful online communities, on which we have extensive data (in many ways, terrorist networks are like geographically dispersed online communities). The technology analyst Chris Allen does a good job of analyzing optimal group size with his work on the Dunbar number.

His analysis (replete with examples) shows that there is a gradual falloff in effectiveness of online groups at 80 members, with an absolute falloff at 150 members. The initial falloff occurs, according to Allen, because of an increasing amount of effort spent on "grooming" the group to maintain cohesion. The absolute falloff occurs at 150 members, when grooming fails to stem dissatisfaction and dissension within the group. This will cause the group to cleave apart into smaller subgroups (although some may remain affiliated with the original group).

Al-Qaeda may have grown much larger than this when it ran a physical training camp in Afghanistan. Physical proximity in a permissive environment allowed the organization to operate as a hierarchy along military lines, complete with the middle management needed to scale beyond 150 members (or at least a mix of hierarchy inside Afghanistan and a distributed network outside the country). Once these camps were broken apart by the U.S.-sponsored invasion (as well as by the assassination of key individuals), the Dunbar limits on group size began to have an effect and caused the fragmentation that is well reported on today.

This leads us to optimal group size, which according to Allen's analysis on online groups can be seen at two levels: small and medium sized. Small, viable (in the sense that they can be effective at a large number of tasks) groups or cells are optimized at seven to eight members. A lower boundary for this can be seen at five, since groups of fewer than five members don't have the diversity in skill sets to be effective at tasks. There is an upper boundary of nine members.

Medium-sized groups are optimally effective at forty-five to fifty members, with a lower limit of twenty-five and an upper limit of eighty. Between the levels of nine and twenty-five, there is a chasm that needs to be surmounted at significant peril to the group. This is due to the need for groups above nine members to have some level of specialization of function. This specialization requires too much management oversight to be efficient if the group is any smaller than twenty-five, given the limited number of participants able to support a functional specialty. At twenty-five members, the group gains a positive return on specialization, given the management effort applied (a break-even point).

This chasm nicely matches the problem period in the development of terrorist and guerrilla networks that studies of guerrilla groups refer to—during the transition from small to medium group size, guerrilla groups are very vulnerable to disruption (which gives credibility to those military strategists who claimed that the United States didn't have a sufficient number of troops in Iraq during the war). Why would groups grow? The reason is that the amount of damage a small five- to seven-member group can do has traditionally been limited, in both scale and narrow geographies. Once a group reaches forty-five to fifty members, it can mount large attacks across multiple geographies.

Groups this size are also very difficult to eliminate because of the geographical dispersion of cells.

This size dynamic can also be seen in criminal organizations. The U.S. mafia, despite its widespread influence, has closely mirrored the limits on group size:

- The Genovese family, which was the largest of the five families in New York City, had a total of 152 members.
- The Gambino family had a terrible year from 2000 to 2001, losing 33 members, but it still managed to retain 130, making it the second largest in manpower.
- The Lucchese family had 113 members, which puts it at number three.

AFGHANISTAN'S ENTREPRENEURS

Recognizing the proliferation of global guerrillas, states will become more and more likely to recruit them as temporary allies, usually for profit as much as for a cause. Fighting fire with fire is an irresistible tactic, and one we're likely to see much more of, as traditional warfare becomes unfeasible. In fact, we've already seen this in the Afghan war. Governments have always been eager to find proxies, but it has never been as easy as it is fast becoming.

Afghanistan's Taliban wasn't a government in the sense that we understand it. It was a loose association along feudal lines. Nonetheless, the senior clerics of the Taliban did exert power. One area of specific focus for the Taliban was the elimination of opium farming.

The remoteness of Afghanistan's valleys and the fierceness of its people made the country the perfect place for opium farming. In 1999, Afghanistan produced 75 percent of the world's supply. In 2000, however, Mohammed Omar, the Taliban's top cleric, banned the production of opium. This was followed by a fatwa that specified opium cultivation as contrary to the edicts of Islam. To enforce this edict, Taliban militias burned heroin labs and jailed farmers until they ceased growing opium. Over one thousand mullahs, farmers, and village elders were jailed in one province alone.

The effect was dramatic. By 2001, the vast majority of Afghanistan's opium crop had been eradicated. The only area left under cultivation in any meaningful way was the 5 percent of the territory under the control of the Western-supported Northern Alliance. In the words of Karim Rahimi, the United Nations drug control liaison in Jelalabad (during the Taliban's rule), "It is amazing, really, when you see the fields that last year were filled with poppies and this year there is wheat."[2]

What the Taliban didn't understand is that the ban on opium production had eliminated the support of a large number of Afghans. Overnight, billions of dollars in revenue that fueled the livelihood of over two million people were eliminated. Most important, it alienated the affections of powerful warlords—Afghanistan's guerrilla entrepreneurs.

When the United States decided to support the Northern Alliance before it attacked the Taliban in early 2002, U.S. officials took action to ensure this disaffection. Direct payments from Central Intelligence Agency operatives and the potential of unfettered opium production under the Northern Alliance exerted a powerful influence on Afghanistan's guerrilla entrepreneurs. This worked. The warlords didn't rise to support the Taliban or its al-Qaeda allies when the U.S. attack began. As a result, the Taliban's few stalwart believers quickly fell in the face of carpet bombing and direct pressure from the ground.

Less than two years later, the guerrilla entrepreneurs were back in business. Poppy production soared to new, unprecedented levels. By 2005, nearly 90 percent of the world's opium was being produced in Afghanistan. This production generated $2.5 billion a year or nearly half the country's gross domestic product (GDP).

A MODERN VENEER ON ANCIENT MIND-SETS

We who live in the real world are aware that literacy, mass communications, urbanization, the spread of engineering train- ing, the internet and other developments have contributed to what social scientists call "social and political mobilization." The peoples of the world are not illiterate villagers anymore, as they largely were in the heyday of the British Raj. They aren't politically helpless and they won't put up with foreign- ers "policing" them, not for very long.

—Juan Cole, a historian of the Middle East and
the author of the blog Informed Comment[3]

Rapid modernization (both economic integration and technological progress) has radically changed the struc- ture, the capabilities, and the constituency of the terrorist groups we face today. The pools of talent that today's ter- rorist groups can draw on are substantially more edu- cated, connected, and mobile than ever before in recorded history. There is ample evidence that this general improve- ment is reflected in the quality of terrorist recruits—pov- erty and a lack of education are not positively correlated with involvement in terrorism and may even be negatively correlated.[4] We aren't facing your father's uneducated, immobile, and poor rice paddy farmer.

But modernization hasn't changed the fundamental associations and interests that drive people. Modern tech- nology has just been layered over already existing familial, tribal, ethnic, and national allegiances. It's just new means put to the same old ends.

In his paper "The New Warrior Class," Ralph Peters provides some insight into this. He defines the term *warrior* as "erratic primitives of shifting allegiance, habituated to violence, with no stake in civil order." He goes on to say:

> We have entered an age in which entire nations are subject to dispossession, starvation, rape, and murder on a scale approaching genocide—not at the hands of a conquering foreign power but under the guns of their neighbors. Paramilitary warriors—thugs whose talent for violence blossoms in civil war—defy legitimate governments and increasingly end up leading governments they have overturned. This is a new age of warlords, from Somalia to Myanmar/Burma, from Afghanistan to Yugoslavia.[5]

He even provides a classification system for these warriors:

- **Underclass.** Losers with little education, no earning power, and no future.
- **Disrupted young males.** Young men and boys drawn into the warrior milieu because of the disruption of normal paths of development (school, work, and so forth).
- **Believers.** Men who fight because of strong religious or patriotic beliefs or those who have suffered extreme personal loss.
- **Former military men.** Former soldiers who have not been reintegrated back into society.

According to Peters, the central paradox of the warrior culture is that these warriors continue conflict for their own gain—the spoils of war and the continuation of a way of life. Perversely, the continuation of violence prevents society from delivering the benefits necessary to rehabilitate them. The truth of who we are facing is somewhere in between Juan Cole's enlightened world that yearns to be free of Western domination and Peters's erratic warriors.

My conclusion is that globalization is quickly layering new skill sets on ancient mind-sets. Warriors, in our current context of global guerrillas, are not merely lazy and monosyllabic primitives as Peters implies. They are wired, educated, and globally mobile. They build complex supply chains, benefit from global money flows, travel globally, innovate with technology, and attack shrewdly. In a nutshell, they are modern. Despite this apparent modernity and an eager willingness to adopt technology, however, their value sets are often completely different from those we find acceptable in the West.

In short, these modern warriors fight for reasons we don't quite understand. Tribal loyalties, clan ties, religious reasons, and more are the basis of their moral cohesion as a group. These beliefs make it difficult, if not impossible, for them to fully integrate into the modern world.

Additionally, they do have a strong motivation to survive. This quest for survival, at any cost, has led them to push into areas that increase their chances of viability. Some have opted to create an alternative system, or protostates, that conform to their values. We have seen this in Hezbollah and Hamas. Others, and this is the group that is on the rise, have opted to move with alacrity into transnational crime.

Guerrilla entrepreneurs, as I have described them in this chapter, are the central actors in this move toward sustainable nonstate entities. They provide innovation in warfare, leverage sources of moral cohesion to grow the group through fictive kinship, find new sources of income through integration with transnational criminality, and much more.

THE TERRORIST SOCIAL SYSTEM

If these global guerrillas aim to hollow out the state, or share power with it, wouldn't we see more terrorists hoping to take on governmentlike duties? Again, we already have.

At the end of the twentieth century, the evolved form of the nonstate entity was the protostate. Since the nation-state system was still fairly dominant, it makes sense that these new entities copied the old model and made it their own. These new terrorist social networks thrived in the vacuum created by failed states.

A good example of this is Hamas (which is serving as a model for Muqtada al-Sadr in Iraq). Since its founding in 1987, Hamas has proven to be a well-run counterweight to the late Yasser Arafat's corrupt Palestinian Authority (which in many ways is the Palestinian state). Hamas runs the following services:

- An extensive education network
- Distribution of food to the poor
- Youth camps and sports
- Elderly care
- Funding of scholarships and business development
- Religious services
- Public safety
- Health care

This network of social services provides Hamas with multiple benefits, including:

- Popular support that shelters the organization
- A plentiful supply of recruits for its terrorist mission
- Sources of external funding through charity organizations that support its social mission (much of which can be redirected to the terrorist mission) and funding through a small number of profitable businesses

The rise of terrorist social services indicates that the loose networks that power terrorist military organizations can also replicate the social responsibilities of nation-states. As a challenger to the nation-state system, this capability speaks volumes. It has also yielded a form of success. Despite a decentralized, almost nonexistent command structure, Hamas won electoral control of Palestine in early 2006. Given the array of forces arranged against it, this assumption of power is likely to fail. It will be faced with the same weaknesses that made states vulnerable in the first place.

TRANSNATIONAL CRIME

You can take their blood; then why not take their property?

—Bakar Bashir, the spiritual head of Jemaah Islamiyah[6]

The more robust, twenty-first-century model for survivability is based on the combination of guerrilla groups and transnational crime. Both have a similar set of goals—ineffectual governments to work around—and are quickly developing similar, twenty-first-century networks. Especially as proxy wars proliferate, the line between the two will blur.

One of the best sources for insight into the rapid growth of transnational crime is Moisés Naím's book *Illicit: How Smugglers, Traffickers, and Copycats Are Hijacking the Global Economy.* Naím comes to the topic of transnational crime with immeasurable experience and insight. When his book came out, I was quick to send him a note of congratulations. For me, it was totally in sync with my work on global guerrillas. Interestingly, he responded that he had seen my op-ed in the *New York Times*[7] on open-source war and had intended to send me a similar note. We've shared quite a few e-mails since then, replete with the shorthand communication of two people who have come to many of the same unpopular conclusions.

In his book, Naím copiously documents how globalization and unrestricted interconnectivity have led to the rise of vast global smuggling networks. These networks live in the spaces between states. They are simultaneously everywhere and nowhere. They make money through an arbitrage (riskless trading that takes advantage of differences in prices for the same exact item in two locations) of the differences between the legal systems and the level of law enforcement of our isolated islands of sovereignty. To make this even easier, they use the vast profits of their operations to overwhelm underpaid government employees with floods of corruption. This allows them to take control of otherwise functional states. You would be surprised, Naím wrote in an e-mail to me, how little it costs to buy an entire government in most parts of the world. Of course, after seeing how little Jack Abramoff spent to corrupt the operation of the U.S. government over the last decade, I am not at all surprised.

By all accounts, the amount of money involved is immense. In aggregate, these networks form a parallel "black" global supply chain, have a GDP of $1 to $3 trillion (some estimates have put this as high as 10 percent of the legal global economy), and are growing at seven times the rate of legal global trade. These networks supply the huge demand in the developed world for:

- Drugs (both recreational and pharmaceutical knock-offs)
- Undocumented workers (for corporations, home services, and the sex trade)
- Weapons (from small arms to rocket-propelled grenades, much of it from cold war arsenals)

- Intellectual property rip-offs (from digital content to brand-named consumer items)
- Money (laundered and unregulated financial flows)

Interestingly, these supply chains aren't run by the vertically integrated cartels and families of the twentieth century (those hierarchies are too vulnerable, slow, and unresponsive to be competitive in the current environment). Instead, they are undifferentiated structures (think Lego blocks) that are highly decentralized, horizontal, and fluid. Their specialization, to the extent that there is one, is in cross-border movement; therefore, they can handle all types of smuggling simultaneously (for example, putting both knockoffs of DVDs and drugs into the backpack of an illegal alien crossing the border). Finally, they are also very quick to adopt new technologies to improve the speed and coordination of their global networks.

Across the board, we are starting to see global guerrillas move into transnational crime. According to Drug Enforcement Administration statistics, nearly half of the forty-one groups on the U.S. government's list of terrorist organizations are involved in drug trafficking—from the Taliban in Afghanistan, which provided protection for opium smuggling, to the guerrillas in Nigeria, who operate multibillion-dollar oil smuggling (bunkering) rings. This growth has been staggering. David Kaplan of *U.S. News & World Report* gets to the point:

> The terrorists behind the Madrid attacks were major drug dealers, with a network stretching from Morocco through Spain to Belgium and the Netherlands. Their ringleader, Jamal "El Chino" Ahmidan, was the brother of one of Morocco's top hashish traffickers. Ahmidan and his followers paid for their explosives by trading hashish and cash with a former miner. When police raided the home of one plotter, they seized 125,800 ecstasy tablets—one of the larg-

est hauls in Spanish history. In all, authorities recovered nearly $2 million in drugs and cash from the group. In contrast, the Madrid bombings, which killed 191 people, cost only about $50,000. . . .

What is new is the scale of this toxic mix of jihad and dope. Moroccan terrorists used drug sales to fund not only the 2004 Madrid attack but the 2003 attacks in Casablanca, killing 45, and attempted bombings of U.S. and British ships in Gibraltar in 2002. So large looms the North African connection that investigators believe jihadists have penetrated as much as a third of the $12.5 billion Moroccan hashish trade—the world's largest—a development worrisome not only for its big money but for its extensive smuggling routes through Europe.[8]

THE ENEMY DEFINED

The growing tide of instability caused by transnational crime–fueled, systems disrupting sons of global fragmentation described in this book will require changes in how we think about security. Conventional approaches, particularly those that rely on centralized nation-state-driven solutions, won't work. These cumbersome, and increasingly limited, initiatives will only cause havoc. Rather, it will require an approach that works with the tide of history by leveraging the organic forces unleashed by our open global platform. For it is only through the power of decentralized action by superempowered groups that lasting stability can be achieved. We have two choices: we can enable its emergence, or we can delay it until it evolves on its own out of necessity.

8

RETHINKING SECURITY

We won the cold war against the Soviet Union by doing two things: a preservation of the status quo without resorting to nuclear warfare and the construction of a global system that radically increased the wealth of its participants.

Security within the twenty-first century will require a new balance between wealth creation and safety. Traditionally, that meant balancing the protection afforded by the state with personal freedoms. It's different today. The balance is increasingly between preserving the benefits of global interconnectivity and insulating against the myriad threats that can strike at us through those same connections.

This is going to require a new approach. As we have seen, the nation-state is not well suited to provide a sole mechanism for that balance to develop. It is slow and cumbersome, and its lethargic response will be similar to that of Microsoft to the many threats to Windows since the advent of the Internet.

Despite this, we have to adapt. If we do not, our security will only deteriorate from here on out. The technological leverage afforded individuals to conduct warfare will continue to increase. Additionally, there are also systemic and naturally occurring threats that loom in the near future. These include avian flu (and pandemics in general), peak oil (that is, when the supply of a nonrenewable resource reaches the natural limit of production), and global warming. If you think these threats are unrelated to what I am talking about in this book, think again.

All these threats are made worse because of the power afforded by rampant global interconnectivity. For example, a pandemic spreads as fast as global travel can take it. With each passing year, the volume of air travel increases and with it the speed and breadth of a pandemic. Our current security system relies on the nation-state to defend us against this eventuality, but it relies on a single point of failure: the national border. It should be assumed that this border will be quickly breached and that state and local governments will be forced to shoulder the bulk of the response. Given everything I have been able to gather on the subject, they haven't taken on any of the preparation necessary to mitigate the impact. For all intents and purposes, we are, as we were on 9/11, defenseless.

To build a solution, we need to start with the assumption that we don't know what the next threat will be. It's clear that new threats will be both amorphous and extremely difficult (nay, impossible) to fully anticipate. Our vulnerabilities are too vast and the sources of potential threat too wide to plan specific defenses against. One thing we can be sure of is that as future attacks occur, they will utilize and be magnified by the deep and growing interconnectivity that now powers our world.

THE BLACK SWAN

There are also unknown unknowns—the ones we don't know we don't know.

—Donald Rumsfeld[1]

A simple way to understand this is to think of these potential attacks as negative system perturbations—or more simply, as black swans, an unexpected negative event that cannot be predicted with any degree of certainty. The time, the target, and the form of the next system perturbations are unknown because they are clouded in uncertainty.

Uncertainty, as opposed to risk, is immeasurable. With risk, we can look at historical data and roughly determine what the potential of a given risk factor's emergence will be in the future. Risk can be managed through hedging and/or additional compensation. For example, if I buy a commodity, there is a risk that the price will drop. That risk can be calculated based on historical performance. I can then buy financial instruments to hedge my downside risk. If I invest in a company, there is a risk that it will fail due to a variety of factors. If I can't hedge this risk, I will often accept contractual remuneration that compensates me for that risk (and I will make outsized returns if the company's stock goes up).

Uncertainty, however, is a different animal. It is based on dark unknowns that have not emerged in historical performance indicators. Uncertainty is problematic. If there is too much uncertainty, financial markets will fail. Money doesn't flow to places where uncertainty makes it impossible to calculate the risk or reward and, in any meaningful way, a potential return. We see the effects of this today in Iraq, where the uncertainty of Iraq's future has driven away investment in its oil industry.

Black swans are uncertain events that have a major effect on markets and systems. In our tightly interconnected world, a black swan can quickly emerge to radically affect the functioning of everything it touches. The best place to go for insight into the theory of black swans is the financial world, where an entire speculation subculture exists for finding ways to profit from unexpected events. Nassim Nicholas Taleb, a scientist, philosopher, and businessman, is a perfect example. He has done some deep thinking on black swans as part of his work in the financial markets.

Taleb saw 9/11 as a black swan, or more precisely, a vicious black swan—an event that couldn't be predicted without any degree of certainty worthy of the label. What's more, he claims that "[a] vicious black swan has an additional elusive property: its very unexpectedness helps create the conditions for it to occur. Had a terrorist attack been a conceivable risk on Sept. 10, 2001, it would likely not have happened."[2]

This is an important point. We are vulnerable because we don't know, and our vulnerability is actually increased because we don't know. Because of this, he argues (correctly), it is easy to engage in hindsight bias. This is the tendency to believe that the event was predictable based on knowledge gained after the event occurred. In effect, people unknowingly substitute current knowledge of outcomes into the gaps of knowledge that were present when building earlier expectations of potential events.

Taleb's analysis reflects the tone of the postmortems that were done after 9/11. There was an incredible focus on the details at the expense of the overall picture. Talk of overlooked memos prevented a deeper level of analysis. There was also lots of focus on organizational failures at the Federal Bureau of Investigation, the Central Intelligence Agency (CIA), and other departments. The problem with all of this, despite how good it feels to point fingers (and it does feel good despite the fact that nobody lost his or her job because of 9/11), is that engaging in hindsight bias doesn't prepare us for the next black swan, the next blip on the horizon that threatens catastrophe.

With the idea of the black swan in our hip pocket, let's search for a solution by first looking at what won't work.

BRITTLE SECURITY

The essence of failure within the realm of security is brittleness. Brittle security fails badly when it fails. It doesn't degrade gracefully or bounce back with new approaches. The following are two examples of brittle security.

Knee-Jerk Police States

As the propagation (particularly those manufactured by globalization's guerrillas) of black swans continues to accelerate, the knee-jerk solution will be to centralize security in the hands of the nation-state. This is a wrongheaded approach. It will bring us to the brink of a police state for very little benefit.

One reason that centralized systems revert to police state measures is that they are outmatched by decentralized and organic threats. These threats gestate below the sensory horizon of the information available to centralized decision makers in a free and open society. To compensate, the state feels forced to develop deeper sources of information through increasingly intrusive methods that generate national-level views of emerging threats. We can already see this in motion as the National Security Agency (NSA) moves to monitor global telephone systems without a warrant or the oversight provided by the Foreign Intelligence Surveillance Act (FISA); the government's mining of Society for Worldwide Interbank Financial Telecomunications financial data; and the government's use of torture and extrajudicial sequestering of suspected terrorists.

In sum, these intrusive methods hurt us more than help us because they run counter to the moral values that have served the United States well in the past. Additionally:

- **They don't generate the information desired.** For example, the NSA's effort to analyze telephone traffic for patterns of usage indicative of terrorism planning doesn't work because patterns of connectivity look similar whether they are for terrorism or for normal business activity (see Valdis Krebs). False positives will vastly outnumber real threat detection. Additionally, torture almost never works as a source of solid information, as the U.S. Army's own field manual on interrogation techniques attests: "Therefore, the use of force is a poor technique, as it yields unreliable results, may damage subsequent collection efforts, and can induce the source to say whatever he thinks the interrogator wants to hear."[3]

- **They reduce domestic and international moral cohesion.** These efforts will run afoul of both domestic groups and international allies. For example, both the NSA's surveillance program and the use of torture have created deep divisions within the U.S. government (domestic cohesion). Some even claim the United States is now in a constitutional crisis because of the Bush administration's circumvention of FISA.

- **They often run afoul of global opinion.** For example, global furor over CIA renditions and the incident at Abu Ghraib have been detrimental to U.S. prestige and alliances (global cohesion). They have also made it much harder for the United States to position itself as a promoter of human rights.

Not only does the centralization of security result in a slide toward police state methods but it also results in unresponsive systems and inefficiencies. Bruce Schneier in *Beyond Fear: Thinking Sensibly about Security in an Uncertain World* cogently argues that centralized security systems such as the U.S. Department of Homeland Security result in a uniformity of methods that make security brittle. In contrast, decentralized security provides a diversity of methods and individual initiative that radically improves overall levels of safety. Additionally, decentralization provides "defense in depth, which means overlapping responsibilities to reduce single points of failure, both for actual defensive matters and intelligence functions."[4]

Preemptive War and Nation-Building

A second approach that is along the wrong path seeks to roll back the external threat—the sources of terrorism and extremism—through the use of preemptive war followed by aggressive nation-building. Interestingly, this approach is currently (in a bastardized form) the grand strategy of the United States (the Bush doctrine). If it were fully realized, it would be closer to what the prolific systems thinker Thomas P. M. Barnett articulates in *The Pentagon's New Map: War and Peace in the 21st Century* and in *Blueprint for Action: A Future Worth Creating*.

In these books, Barnett argues that the United States should lead a coalition of the world's biggest economies to actively manage the expansion of the global market. His approach would institutionalize preemptive war to expand democracy and free markets. Barnett's approach can be seductive given his optimism and his systems thinking, and I doubt I can give it full justice in the space I have allotted it here. Regardless, here's my attempt.

He points out, as I do, that we live in an interconnected world (and to some who've seen a recent online debate we had, we sound like two sides of the same coin). However, rather than assume that global complexity is ungovernable through central means, he takes the opposite approach: that it can be governed and that we can radically improve its operation. In essence, Barnett thinks that it is possible to use military force to improve economic and social connectivity and thereby accelerate the end of history (à la Francis Fukuyama's *The End of History and the Last Man*) and the arrival of a world where everyone is living in a capitalist democracy. His A-to-Z solution includes the following elements:[5]

1. Use the UN Security Council as a grand jury to indict rogue or failed states.
2. A coalition of the biggest economies would issue warrants for the arrest of the offending parties.
3. A warfighting coalition (of the willing) led by the United States would topple the offending state.
4. A competent system administrator (sysadmin) force (modeled after the concept of a computer network system administrator)[6] that includes counterinsurgency experts to first secure the country and reconstruction experts from nations in the developed world to rebuild it (by connecting it to the global economy).
5. The offending leaders would be prosecuted as individuals.

As I said before, Barnett's approach is seductive, and the simplicity of this rule set is an example of this. Unfortunately, it won't work. It is wrong to think that every manufactured and natural system shock that sweeps the global system in the future will originate in failed states of what Barnett calls the "Gap." As we have concluded, black swans are unpredictable. Manufactured black swans, that is, those from globalization's guerrillas, are spreading to new areas. While most of these locations are in the Gap, their reach has spread beyond it to locations in the developed world (for example, the attacks on London and Madrid sprang from indigenous threats). Furthermore, natural black swans, such as the avian flu and other diseases, are as likely to come from a bird population in China (not in the Gap) as anywhere else. Also, while the threat today appears to be mostly Islamic groups, the larger trend line of technological superempowerment will cause this source of instability to shift quickly as the viable group size necessary to declare war on the world drops.

In regard to the sysadmin concept,[7] it is not at all clear that we can improve our ability to pacify and rebuild nations to a level that can actually work. Early tests have produced horrible results in Afghanistan and Iraq. Global guerrillas, as copiously documented in this book, have kept those states in a perpetual condition of failure since the initial invasions by the United States. They have also become havens and sources of even more instability than they were before we invaded.

Another example in our recent experience of a sysadmin capability in action (in a permissive environment on U.S. soil, which should have made it *easy*) is the recovery of New Orleans after Hurricane Katrina devastated it. It was the perfect opportunity to demonstrate that the United States had learned from 9/11 about how to quickly implement efforts that could mitigate the impact of an unexpected event. In short, everything went horribly wrong. It became a management and coordination fiasco. Not only were we unprepared for the effort required to reduce the impact of the event but also we have been slow and unresponsive to the needs of New Orleans to recover from it. The net result is that an American city was destroyed and may never fully recover.

The after-action reports for Katrina focused almost exclusively on the same sort of hindsight biases seen in the post-9/11 reports. They were full of blame and condemnation and not focused on ways to build a more responsive system. The aftermath also pointed to other failures. The

Department of Homeland Security was excessively focused on prevention of terrorism through centralization before the conflict and on bureaucratic control of the deployment of assets during and after the crisis. It is hard to see how this centralized system will produce anything other than disaster in the future.

Another way to look at these wars is as system perturbations[8] that are meant to change the way the Middle East and Central Asia operate. Unfortunately, as we have seen in many other instances with the complex and tightly interconnected system we live in today, it is impossible to foresee the outcomes of system destabilization.

Because this is the primary lesson we've yet to learn from invading Iraq, it is worth repeating: it is impossible to foresee the outcomes of system destabilization. In this case, we wantonly inflicted disruption on ourselves. The loss of over one million barrels of Iraqi oil a day, at the very same moment global demand has reached new highs, has put the global oil system on the edge of shortage. Not only are we paying excessive prices for oil (double what the price was before the war), but we have also become extremely vulnerable to any future events that curtail production in even the slightest way.

The final critique is that it is impossible to fully disengage from a legacy of intense nationalism to create an environment of positivist and clearheaded global decision making. Nationalism continues to creep into this process, whether it comes in the form of gaining economic advantage over competitive nations, fear of U.S. power, or historical enmity. For example, the July 2006 invasion of Lebanon to engage Hezbollah was an exercise in Israeli nationalism in the form of self-protection. It didn't seek to address any of the legitimate concerns that would normally be addressed in neutral problem solving (particularly in regards to territory and security issues). Despite this, the United States quickly turned this conflict into a step forward in its policy of preventive war. The upshot is that the entire enterprise lost legitimacy, and the system perturbation caused the near collapse of a new Middle East democracy in Lebanon.

THE LIMITATIONS OF THE MODERN STATE

> Any community that fails to prepare, with the expectation that the federal government or, for that matter, even the state government will come to their rescue at the final moment will be tragically wrong.
>
> —Michael Leavitt, the secretary of U.S. Health and Human Services, speaking to an audience about avian flu in early 2006[9]

The common thread that dooms these "solutions" to failure is that they rely on the nation-state as the primary actor. Given the speed and complexity posed by the black swans we face, the nation-state would need instantaneous responsiveness, infinite resources, and Godlike insight to be effective.

It has none of these attributes. In the international sphere, the complexity and size of the world outstrips the ability of any single state or even most groups of states to appreciably change it. Furthermore, the increasing diversity of global opinion is making it extremely difficult to achieve any meaningful form of consensus—the response to the threat of global warming comes immediately to mind.

If the U.S. government had the power to predict, fight, and win every war—alone or with help—it would also have the power to predict and stop hurricanes, economic downturns, cancer, and losses in the Olympics. It's simply not possible.

One driver of consensus fragmentation is that every security effort is now analyzed within the context of how it will affect our economic competitiveness. States that willfully ignore this will be at the mercy of those that don't. In a world of unbounded capitalism, Adam Smith's invisible hand (in the form of the self-interest of global currency and bond traders) will mete out swift punishment to those states that take on too many noneconomic burdens. It is likely only a question of time before the twin U.S. deficits (government and trade) prove this point valid. Put simply, in that direction lies financial ruin.

In security, everything is a trade-off.[10] Attempts to use the state to take on any and all security options, from defending all potential targets in the U.S. to remaking the world in its image, is farcical. For security to work, it needs to be:

- **Affordable.** Government-mandated systems and services are unlikely to produce anything within reason that is affordable. A quick look at the U.S. Department of Defense budget supports this. To really build security, it needs to benefit from competitive pressure (to reduce costs), innovation (to increase price and performance), and the vicissitudes of demand (change based on need).
- **Efficiently allocated.** Given the examples of pork and insider dealing in government contracts, this is not even an option if it is centrally controlled. Instead, to be efficient resources must be allocated quickly through a dynamic process that sends them to the correct recipient. Nothing else will work in a world of rapid system shocks.
- **Broad-based and participatory.** By their nature, states desire complete control over security (a de facto security monopoly). This creates a situation of dependence and a sloughing off of responsibility. To be effective, security systems need to involve people at every level.

These requirements are not something that a modern state can accomplish or afford. Additionally, its decision-making process is too flawed, slow, and insular to make the decisions that matter. Given this, it's time to think about a new approach to security: one that meets the requirements of robustness, speed, and efficiency that the new environment requires.

DYNAMIC DECENTRALIZED RESILIENCE

Given our experience, I am ready to call it quits on the highly centralized and overly prescriptive proposals by governing bodies. All the early indications from this approach are pointing toward negative outcomes. In fact, our enemies have already come to the same conclusions and abandoned centralized methods themselves. My belief is that the only way to ensure security in the future will be through survival and decentralized resilience.

A focus on survival and decentralization isn't as simplistic or naive as it seems on first glance. It doesn't mean that we don't pursue criminals, terrorists, and other threats that face us—far from it. The state should pursue these individuals with all the means at its disposal. It also doesn't mean that we should attempt to remake the world in our image or attempt to fight grand battles for the hearts and minds of the world. As we have seen, and will continue to see as long as we pursue this strategy, every attempt we make to build states or wage ideological war will end in greater levels of instability. No, survival requires a new mind-set—or better yet, a philosophy, one that will carry us through the threats we currently face from global guerrillas and oil shocks to threats unimagined along the trend line of technological superempowerment.

So what do I mean by survival? It is simply the ability to dynamically mitigate and dampen system shocks. Specifically, it is those things we (and our state) can do to change the configuration of our networks to ensure that intentional or naturally occurring attacks on our society don't do much damage or spiral out of control. The following are the five tenets of this philosophy.

Thinking in Terms of Market-States and Minimalist Platforms

> In the modern brand of terrorist warfare, what an enemy can do directly is limited. The most dangerous thing it can do is to provoke you into hurting yourself.
>
> —James Fallows[11]

To develop a more robust vision of what it takes to survive (and thrive) globally, the first thing we need to do is rethink our conception of the state. Our traditional approach views the state as a hermetic entity (and able to avoid the aspects of state overstretch mentioned earlier by increasing the levels of mobilization). That clearly isn't the case anymore. Globalization has changed the landscape. States are no longer singular nation-states, but rather (meta?) organizations in competition within a globe-spanning marketplace. This shift is already in the process of changing the character of the state's constitutional order (its source of legitimacy), even though foreign and security policy are still caught in the nation-state phase of thinking.

The best source I have found on how the state is changing is Philip Bobbitt, who is an absolutely brilliant constitutional legal scholar. His book *The Shield of Achilles: War, Peace, and the Course of History* makes a historically detailed case that the bureaucratic nation-state is in an inevitable transition to a more competitive form called the *market-state*. He correctly tags the driver of this change as economics, or more precisely, the emergence of a global superinfrastructure that enables hypercompetitive economic competition. He makes a cogent case that all the major nation-states, from China to the United States to the European Union participants, are in varying phases of this transition.

All these states are struggling with the loss of the core legitimacy of the nation-state—its ability to provide for the welfare of its people. This welfare is both too expensive and too cumbersome to administer within a hyper-competitive atmosphere. As a replacement, these states are in the midst of shifting their legitimacy to deliver maximal "opportunity" through the use of market mechanisms.

There will be differences in how to accomplish this, however.[12] Because the market-state secures political legitimacy through the active pursuit of opportunity for its citizens but declines to specify the goals for which that opportunity is used, there will be different models whose advocates can plausibly maintain that their constitutional strategy best maximizes opportunity.

From this competition, Bobbitt posits that three dominant methods have emerged:

- **The entrepreneurial market-state.** This market-state characterizes the U.S. approach. This model minimizes regulation to increase flexibility of approach and consumer choice. It is characterized by privatized health care, pensions, education, and housing; open immigration; and low taxes.
- **The mercantile market-state.** This is exemplified by Taiwan, Korea, Japan, and Singapore. This approach maximizes employment. To do this, it dictates high savings rates, heavily subsidizes research and development and other types of critical industries, and engineers exchange rates.
- **The managerial market-state.** This describes the European Union. This model maximizes social cohe-

sion. To accomplish this, it uses cooperative relationships between labor and corporations, broad-based social safety nets, and income normalization through taxation.[13]

Each of these protean market-states is in the midst of reworking its constitutional structure to maximize the opportunity of its respective population. We can expect that during this transition phase there will be mistakes, reversals, and revisions in each of the respective approaches as a dispassionate global marketplace adjudicates their efficacy. Furthermore, and most important for our purposes, there will be a profound sense of vulnerability and lack of legitimacy for major states during this period.

In general, the primary source of conflict between market-states, given their emerging makeup, will not be ideological, but economic. This stands to reason, given that all of them have adopted the same system, one that is driven by economic competition. Despite this similarity, the differences in style can result in conflict. Bobbitt details three examples of complaints that could lead to conflict:

- Mercantile—"exploiting foreign markets while closing their own [not open enough]"
- Entrepreneurial—"failure to get control of consumption and thus exporting inflation [too chaotic]"
- Managerial—"keeping interest rates high [not growing fast enough]"[14]

While it is possible that these complaints could lead to conflict, as trade issues helped bring the United States and Japan to war in World War II, it is unlikely in the current context that these factors would be sufficient for warfare. The most likely factor that could lead to warfare is something that Bobbitt doesn't fully address in his book but that we have seen ample evidence of in the early part of the twenty-first century: residual nationalism. Getting past that residual nationalism will be one key to making the world a more survivable place. This is particularly important to do because within it are the seeds of the destruction of the entire global trading system (which has happened before).

So, let's get back to what this means to our survival. Internationally, we need the ability to do the following to improve the chances that our trading system will survive the application of residual nationalism (adventurism, ideological crusades, overreaction, selfishness, and so forth). To do this, we need to build a mechanism that ensures that the global system of trade and communication doesn't suffer damage or complete collapse as tensions inevitably rise. This is in stark contrast to the plethora of calls by otherwise intelligent strategists for the establishment of new organizations to increase activism, which as we have seen will likely backfire to create more disorder.

The best approach to accomplishing this is to copy something we have seen recently in a phenomenon that has swept the globe: the Internet. The Internet wasn't planned by nation-states or by groups of nations. It grew organically based on simple rules of construction. The beauty of the system, and the key to its success, was that it was a minimalist rule set. It wasn't complex at its core, although the network became extremely complex and robust over time.

The minimalist rule set that translates the experience we gained from the Internet into a working model is a focus on trade. Within this new minimalist model, open trade and communications are key. Open trade and communications rip down borders and ideologies and are pure poison to real warfare. Over time, they will cure most ills. The key is to give them time to work.

This isn't as simplistic as it sounds (I find I am going to have to say this a lot), nor is it something that has been already occurring in the way it should. The collapse of the Doha Round of the World Trade Organization (WTO) and recent moves to limit the use of the Internet in China are two good examples of this. Too often, trade and communications have become slaves of nationalism (for examples, the disconnection of Cuba and Iran). They are subject to the maximal rule sets of politics, history, wealth protection (in the form of copyrights and patents), and ill-conceived foreign and security policy. To succeed in transforming the global system into something that is robust and survivable, we need to put these concerns to the side and focus on the strict application of the minimalist rules necessary to grow communications and trade transaction volume at the greatest rate.

The flip side of a focus on simple rules (which, if history serves as a guide, are the only rules a vast number of participants can agree on) is that the application of these rules must be jealously guarded, and the interests of the system, as an entity unto itself, should be protected. Here's where it gets interesting. This calls for the establishment of a body that oversees the global marketplace: a society of economic engineers that is focused on ensuring that the members of the system adhere to the simple rules that form its basis for being and that points out system design problems that can result in future failures for all or part of the network.

In short, this isn't the WTO. The WTO isn't focused on the care of the system. Instead, it is in almost all cases focused on national issues and on competitive advantage and can be expected to be a relentless advocate of its peculiar maximal rule set. As many critics point out about the North American Free Trade Agreement, the Central

American Free Trade Agreement, the WTO, and the like, if they were really agreements about free trade, they would be less than a page long. Instead, the WTO needs to be focused on the propagation and continued success of the system itself and have the means to enforce actions that protect it (within the field of global economics and communication, this oversight body will look more like a standards enforcement body than any political entity). Changes and alterations to the core rule sets will need to be almost unanimous among participants, in a fashion as difficult as amending the U.S. Constitution.

Granted, I will concede that this is a tall order and something totally foreign to most readers. There will be those, and they will be legion, who will contend that the complexity of global trade and communications makes simple rules of interaction impossible. There will also be some who claim that sovereignty is something that should trump the global system in all cases. I would counter by saying that complexity, and we have many examples of this, can be built from simple rules and that this system would be entirely voluntary; as such, sovereignty can be maintained by simply withdrawing from it.

Can it be done in the near to medium term? I don't know. However, as connectivity continues to grow and system shocks sow doubt among participating states about the wisdom of participating in the system, something like the body I describe here will be built. It's likely inevitable. Perhaps it will take a severe retrenchment in trade and cross-communications (significant damage) to make us realize how much we have lost.

Regardless of whether this common framework for connectivity is built or not in the near to medium term, our quest for survival through deep resilience doesn't stop there. We still need to build systems that provide a dampening or mitigation of systems shocks. To build these systems, we need to think in terms of platforms.

Thinking in Terms of Platforms

Let's start with an example. My interactions with the dedicated members of the Terrorist Early Warning Group in Los Angeles demonstrate to me that they are building on the right kind of approach. They are coordinating, training, and practicing those skills necessary to deal with potential events, whatever they may be. With the advent of additional disruptions, the efforts we see in New York City and Los Angeles will go nationwide as people begin to take security into their own hands.

Their access to the critical funds and resources necessary to make this happen, however, is less than limited—it is embarrassing. Currently, only 0.1 percent of all federal security funding is transferred to the states and local governments for terrorism and disaster prevention. In fact, this money is being cut for some of the most vulnerable locations like New York City and Los Angeles.

These local organizations are also finding it difficult to coordinate their activities with federal agencies. The national security culture of secrecy has made impossible all but the most basic of information sharing and collaboration. In desperation and deep lack of trust (spawned by a failure of notification before 9/11 and since then), these organizations have had to build their own parallel organizations to provide much of the information they should be getting from federal sources.

To reverse this downward spiral, we need to decentralize our efforts. The best way to accomplish this, as demonstrated in both industry and technology, is to build a platform that fosters the development of local innovation.

Here's how a platform works. A platform is merely a collection of services and capabilities that are common to a wide variety of activities aggregated in a way that makes them exceedingly easy to access. The benefit of this approach is that it becomes easier for end users of this platform to build solutions because they don't need to re-create the wheel in order to build a new service, and it is easier for participants to coordinate and interconnect their activities.

Here's an example from the Internet on how innovation can occur on a platform. Tallinn, Estonia, isn't a likely place for a revolution of innovation. It's a backwater. A rump state left over from the breakup of the Soviet Union. The decayed infrastructure belies its true nature: it's the perfect place to foment a revolution under the radar of the establishment. This revolution takes the form of Tallinn's best-known company: Skype. It's a company and a software program that allows people to talk to one another, anywhere in the world, using just a computer and an Internet connection. Best of all, it's free—just the thing to break a natural monopoly.

In only two years after making it available, Skype's motley collection of programmers are presiding over 150,000 downloads a day. Each download costs less than half a cent to connect (a tiny fraction of traditional telephone customer acquisition costs), and with over 44 million registered users, it has a phone system as big as most countries. Not only is it remaking the map of telephony but it is also making money. Since its founding, Skype has made over $18 million on reasonably priced premium services.

The secret of Skype's success isn't the innovative method of personal computer–to–personal computer communication and the simplicity of design it developed, although these played a part. It also isn't merely that it is free or runs without a costly large central network. These advantages would have been impossible to introduce if Skype wasn't able to leverage the global platforms of the technology industry and the Internet.

Platform providers from Microsoft to Intel to the collection of companies that form the Internet provide Skype with the underlying services that make it work. Precisely because it doesn't have to replicate the feature functionality of already-deployed software and networks, it can focus on those things that truly add value. Skype isn't alone—corporate successes from Google to eBay have leveraged this same core functionality to revolutionize their target markets.

This monstrously complex, mutually dependent network of companies, technologies, and functionality works together (more or less) to provide the platforms Skype needs to deliver its groundbreaking innovation from its headquarters in Estonia. This new world of globally integrated technology is very different from that of the vertically integrated information technology solutions providers of two decades ago (just as the new security environment is different from the vertically integrated security arrangements that dominated the twentieth century).

While this example of a platform is from a commercial and technological market, it provides us clues on how to build and develop platforms that enhance our survival. To see what this means in action, let's create a set of attributes common to platforms and then apply them to real-life situations. The following is the short list of platform attributes:

- **Transparency.** Platform mechanisms, both static and dynamic, must be viewable by external parties.
- **Two way.** All the participants connected by the platform must have the ability to interact with it as both a consumer and a provider of services (both demand and supply).

- **Openness.** The platform must be open to all comers, in that any and all parties that want to provide innovations should be able to access the system to do so.

With this philosophy of platforms in place, we can apply it to a system that underpins our survival: the electricity system.

This system is critical to almost all modern societies in the age of computers. It is also a prime target for any global guerrillas intent on disrupting a society—as we have seen again and again in Iraq. Despite this, the electricity system is merely a distribution network and not a platform with intrinsic resilience. To change this, we need to add platform characteristics to the electricity network. The simple first step is to make it a truly two-way system.

Despite improvements in the ability of individuals to produce power locally (primarily through solar), local production is still difficult and expensive. Furthermore, underinvestment in the electrical grid over the last decades has not kept pace with a rapid growth of peak demand. We continually find ourselves on the edge of rolling brownouts (as most people in California and New York City can attest to after experiencing the summers of the last decade) and being much more vulnerable to black swan events as we approach self-organizing criticality. Furthermore, the quality of the power has been neglected—which is poison in a world of computers—to the extent that we spend $100 billion a year on replacements to all damaged equipment connected to the grid in the U.S. alone.

The simple solution that enhances survivability is to turn the electricity system into a platform. The first step to doing this is to make the power system truly two way. This critical change, made possible by market incentives (which is the only mechanism a market-state has to generate rapid change), should allow any individual on the network to become both a producer and a consumer of the product. The interconnection for this must be plug-dumb—in that it should be as simple as merely plugging any local production into the system to get credit for the effort. This approach makes it possible for individuals to produce excess power during the day to generate credits for usage at night (which eliminates the need for local storage).

To really make this zoom, the pricing structure for buying power must be changed to become more transparent. This means that power companies need to be restructured from market makers of power (an opaque process of buying low and selling high, despite regulation) into a manager of transmission networks that provides services to those who connect to it. The power companies would provide market spot prices (the more fluid the better) and net a minimal management fee for transmission for power that individuals and companies contribute to it. If these changes were put into effect, it is easy to envision that local power production would blossom as individuals and companies rush to participate.

A final change would be to improve the openness of the system to outside service providers. This change would allow companies to connect to the grid to provide value-added services to the power system such as power conditioning and local storage for resiliency against blackouts. In this way, towns and cities could buy services that enhance their local competitiveness and quality of life.

If looked at in aggregate, transforming the power system into a platform will have a substantial effect on our resilience and survivability. Not only will we enjoy immediate benefits but also we will enhance the complexity of the system in ways that radically improve its ability to withstand system shocks through the geographic distribution of production, local and regional value-added services, and the elimination of single points of failure.

Another stopping point in our emerging philosophy of resilience and survivability is to think in terms of what platforms spawn: ecosystems.

Thinking in Terms of Ecosystems

I had the fortune of being introduced to business ecosystems through my work with Marco Iansiti, a Harvard Business School professor and author. The experience clicked with me because I viewed business in a similar way. How does this apply to our discussion of survivability?

If we take the power system platform example from the previous section, we will see that over time this system will develop a complex and interdependent network of companies and individuals that provide it new products, services, and sources of demand. This larger network, which is built on the basis of a new open platform, is what Iansiti and others call an ecosystem.

From the standpoint of survivability, ecosystem health is a critical factor in the ability of this system to produce societal and economic resilience. To really understand this, let's dive into Iansiti's thinking on this. In *The Keystone Advantage,* Iansiti and Roy Levien maintain that an ecosystem is a large, complex, and loosely connected network of companies and individuals that share the same fate. This "shared fate" is the result of codependencies that derive from the presence of modularity and platforms in the network. While complex interdependencies have existed in industries for some time, the advent of the Internet has raised the level of interdependence several orders of magnitude.

In measuring the effectiveness and health of ecosystems, Iansiti and Levien provide the following criteria:

- **Productivity.** Is the ecosystem generating improvements in productivity as measured by factor productivity, time, and delivery of innovation?

- **Robustness.** Do ecosystem participants share a high survival rate? Is the ecosystem structure maintained after system shocks? Is there continuity in product viability (via limited obsolescence) and user experience?
- **Niche creation.** Is there an increase in variety by both firm type and products and technologies?[15]

So, if we can measure ecosystem health, what will we do if we find dysfunctional ecosystems? The answer comes in two parts. The first is to determine the cause of the dysfunction and the second is to use the only real tool of market-states: market incentives.

In determining the cause of ecosystem dysfunction, Iansiti and Levien's analysis is again useful. They find through copious analysis that the usual cause of ecosystem failure (as per the previously mentioned criteria) is due to the presence of two types of firms (or in a more general sense, participants):[16]

- The landlord dominates a critical hub position in the network. "Landlords follow a fundamentally inconsistent strategy. They refuse to integrate forward to control assets that are crucial to their operation. However, they extract so much value from the ecosystem that they make the business models of the needed niche firms unsustainable."[17] An example of this is Enron.
- The dominator vertically integrates into all aspects of the ecosystem. "Dominator firms are firms that control both value capture and value creation in the ecosystem domain . . . often producing closed architectures that eliminate the possibility of other firms leveraging, building on, and extending their products."[18] Examples include the early days of IBM, DEC, and AT&T.

If either of these firm types is seen within an ecosystem, it is almost certain that it will produce levels of fragility that make it unusable as a protection against system shocks. To correct this, market-states and their constituent organizations (from private to public) must work diligently to provide market-based incentives for these firms to change their behavior. The objective of this effort is to get key hub players in the emerging network to act as keystones.[19] These firms or organizations follow a strategy that focuses on the growth of the ecosystem as well as on the firm itself. It does this by:

- Creating high-value sharable assets
- Creating and managing physical and information hubs
- Supporting uniform standards (open connections)
- Creating and packaging state-of-the-art tools and building blocks for innovation
- Maintaining performance standards
- Acquiring financial assets for operating leverage
- Reducing uncertainty by centralizing communications
- Reducing complexity by supporting and providing powerful platforms[20]

In every case of where we deploy platforms to improve our resilience to system shocks, we need to ensure that the organization that is managing this central position adopts a keystone strategy. This applies regardless of whether it is a private firm, a nongovernmental organization, a government agency, or an individual who occupies this position.

In almost all cases today, we see dominator and landlord organizations across almost all areas of security and resilience. This applies to the Department of Defense, to electricity and gas firms, the WTO, and the producers and distributors of oil. As a result, the level of innovation and robustness we see in the networks we are provided by these organizations is paltry, nonexistent, or in retreat. Furthermore, the dysfunctional nature of these networks will make it a certainty that as foreseeable threats crop up in the future, we will not take the measures necessary to ensure that the ecosystem prebuilds the capacity to mitigate their impact.

Thinking in Terms of Open-Source Networks That Work on Our Behalf

In earlier chapters of this book, I've put the role of open-source networks in the camp of global guerrillas. They certainly shouldn't have a monopoly on this form of organization. Open-source networks—networks that are defined by open access, sharing, collective effort, and diversity of motive—have a major role to play in building and maintaining our resilience to threats.

Open source has already demonstrated its ability to transform the software industry by creating, building, and delivering products of extreme usefulness. Within areas of survival, open source can play a role in rapidly building collectives of concerned individuals, corporations, and other organizations to address specific problems. To really get a sense of what these organizations are capable of within this role, let's refer to the work of Calvert Jones and Sarai Mitnick[21] on how open-source networks improved our ability to respond to both Hurricane Katrina and the Southeast Asian tsunami.

In each case, networks were built online to provide a gathering point for a diverse set of participants. A combination of software (blogs and wikis) was used to construct hubs for information sharing, coordination, and offerings and/or requests for help, services, and goods. These sites played an extremely important adjunct to the centralized efforts of states to respond to the crises. Interestingly, as with most open-source efforts, the organizers of these sites were relative unknowns. They began their efforts out of concern, and as the need for help grew, they attracted a wide variety of strangers to help. These outsiders collectively self-organized into divisions of labor that enabled the sites to grow to meet the challenges of maintaining them.

Unfortunately, in each case the efforts of these people were relatively unrecognized by the state sources of global wealth and power. States did not offer services, money, or other forms of support (even recognition). Furthermore, it is unlikely that these efforts will get the necessary funding to capture and/or retain the lessons learned during these events so that they can be leveraged in the future as needed.

The philosophical point here, in regard to how it could help our survivability in the future, is to pressure organizations to which we belong (including market-states, corporations, charities, and so forth), to participate, support, and sustain these open-source efforts. It is possible, if this approach is followed, to find that in the future we will have a plethora of unexpected robust capabilities by which we can dynamically allocate the resources we need to prevent and respond to black swans that emerge.

Thinking in Terms of Sustainability Instead of Dependence

Besides the improvements in how we design and operate our critical systems, we also need to change the way we approach consumption. Western society, in aggregate, operates on a just-in-time consumption basis. While this is advantageous in terms of variety and efficiency, it is dangerously vulnerable to systems disruption. Just-in-time consumption can quickly break down if the costs of energy used to transport these goods increase radically, the concentrated global sources of these goods are plunged into chaos, or the transportation system itself is disrupted (think in terms of the airport panics in response to terrorism threats). Furthermore, this situation is made even worse by a tightening of supply because of an exponential growth in global demand for these resources generated by the emergence of over two billion Chinese and Indian consumers—it is important to understand that with exponential growth, when half of the supply's reserves are consumed, you are only one doubling cycle from complete depletion.

To correct this situation, we need to make sustainability a critical part of everything we do at the individual and group levels. Fortunately, the environmentalist community has pioneered many of the methods we will need to make this transition (albeit largely for different reasons). This community demonstrates that sustainable living is possible without giving up all the features and benefits of modern existence. Most critically, the plethora of products and businesses that have been introduced over the last decades from this community is a clear demonstration that sustainable living can become a marketplace-driven activity that increases material and personal well-being rather than a futile effort of self-deprivation.

Following are a couple of examples. One of the most critical and vulnerable dependencies we have is our dependence on external sources of energy. We cannot, on the whole, live without connections to our global resource of supply chains that provide us with electricity, natural gas, and oil. One frequently touted solution to reducing that vulnerability is to find ways to produce energy within our national borders. However, that approach falls short of where we need to be. It still makes us vulnerable to the disruption of the interregional transportation of these resources (for example, the Alaskan oil pipeline, natural gas pipelines from the Gulf of Mexico, and high-voltage transmission lines from Washington State to California). A more resilient approach to sustainability requires a focus on the local production of energy.

That approach makes the suburban home the unit of focus. It is a place where rapidly improving technologies in areas such as geothermal heating and cooling; solar hot water and electricity; and energy-efficient appliances, computers, and lighting are already providing affordable solutions with rapid payback through savings. These improvements are being extended to automobiles, particularly in the long-range fully electric category from companies such as Tesla Motors, which is turning the costs of powering a commute into a small extension of household electricity production. Even in the area of telecommunications, efforts and solutions are under way such as the Green WiFi Project, which will make connecting with core Internet bandwidth and telephone systems fully solar powered. From all these signs of marketplace ingenuity, it's clear that sustainability is coming and that it will cost us much less to operate than it currently does. Perhaps all it will take to turn these innovations from a nice-to-have option to a necessity is to promote them in terms of security, resilience, and survivability.

FINAL THOUGHTS

Because we are unable to decapitate, outsmart, or defend ourselves against global guerrillas, naturally occurring events, and residual nationalism from causing cascades of failure throughout the global system, we need to learn to live with the threat they present. As we have already seen, this doesn't mean an activist foreign policy that seeks to rework the world in our image, police state measures to ensure state security, or spending all of our resources on protecting everything. It does mean the adoption of a philosophy of resilience that ensures that when these events do occur (and they will), we can more easily survive their impact.

By building resilience into the fabric of our daily life, our response to these threats will organically emerge in what seems like an effortless way. Without them, we will suffer the effects of dynamic shocks on a brittle system.[22] With this in mind, I've created a scenario that characterizes what a breakdown looks like to serve as a warning of what we can expect in the future.

9

A BRITTLE SECURITY BREAKDOWN

Regardless of whether or not we can muster the will to build decentralized resilience into our lives, it will arrive.[1] In the near future, if we haven't made any moves toward decentralized security and resiliency, the system will break hard.

Eventually and inevitably, there will be black swan events that directly affect the United States. The first casualty of these events will be the ultrabureaucratic U.S. Department of Homeland Security, which, despite its new extralegal surveillance powers, will prove unable to isolate and defuse the threats against us. (Its one big idea for keeping the global insurgency at bay—building a fence between Mexico and the United States, proposed in a recent congressional immigration bill—will prove as effective as the Maginot Line and the Great Wall of China.) Furthermore, the extra police powers that it will be granted in the wake of these attacks will be counterproductive because these powers will only serve to divide the United States and generate a significant base of domestic dissent and vociferous debate.

But the metaphorical targets of 9/11 are largely behind us. The strikes of the future will be strategic, pinpointing the systems we rely on, and they will leave entire sections of the country without energy and communications for protracted periods. But the frustration and economic pain that result will have a curious side effect: they will spur development of an entirely new, decentralized security system, one that devolves power and responsibility to a mix of local governments, private companies, and individuals. This structure is already visible in the legions of private contractors in Iraq and in New York's amazingly effective counterterrorism intelligence unit. But as we look out toward 2016, the long-term implications are clearer.

Security will become a function of where you live and whom you work for, much as health care is allocated already. Wealthy individuals and multinational corporations will be the first to bail out of our collective system, opting instead to hire private military companies, such as Blackwater and Triple Canopy, to protect their homes and facilities and to establish a protective perimeter around daily life. Parallel transportation networks—evolving out of the time-share aircraft companies such as Warren Buffett's NetJets—will cater to this group, leapfrogging its members from one secure, well-appointed lily pad to the next. Members of the middle class will follow, taking matters into their own hands by forming suburban collectives to share the costs of security—as they do now with education—and shore up delivery of critical services. These "armored suburbs" will deploy and maintain backup generators and communications links; they will be patrolled by civilian police auxiliaries that have received corporate training and boast their own state-of-the-art emergency-response systems. As for those without the means to build their own defense, they will have to make do with the remains of the national system. They will gravitate to the cities, where they will be subject to ubiquitous surveillance and marginal or nonexistent services. For the poor, there will be no other refuge.

Internationally, the mess will be even worse. High oil prices, a significant drop in global economic activity these prices cause, and numerous attacks by global guerrillas will put globalization into retreat. Barriers will emerge against outside threats (both economic and security) along the borders of every major trading bloc. The drop in trade and the inflation this creates will be absorbed badly by most major economies. It will be a disaster within China. The Chinese government lost any residual claim to nation-state legitimacy in the 1990s because of rampant corruption and inattention to the basic needs of its citizens. Its only source of legitimacy was based on market-state norms: economic opportunity and growth. With the decline of global trade, the Chinese bubble economy will go into free fall. Any claims to its one form of legitimacy that formed over the last three decades of scintillating growth will be shattered in less than a year. Mass protests will rise from the 2006 average of two hundred a day to the thousands. Furthermore, these protests will become more violent.

Initially, the Chinese government will try to crack down on these protests through the use of its recently expanded paramilitaries. However, these well-armed irregulars will only exacerbate the violence when they cause several major massacres. As the cycle of violence accelerates, the Chinese military will be rushed in to quell the protests. Without legitimacy, however, Chinese military units will melt away when faced with killing protesters. Several may even join with the protesters to sow regional chaos. With the country in full disintegration, regional and local governments will begin to declare their independence from the central government (and in several cases, with newly installed management). China will finally revert to its historical norm: fragmentation.

Global and local chaos will continue until the next wave of adaptive innovation takes hold. All these changes may prove to be exactly the kind of creative destruction we need to move beyond the current, failed state of affairs. By 2016 and beyond, real long-term solutions will emerge. Cities, which will be the most acutely affected by the new disruptions, will move fastest to become self-reliant, drawing from a wellspring of new ideas the market will put forward. These will range from building-based solar systems by firms such as Energy Innovations to privatized disaster and counterterrorist responses. We will also see the emergence of packaged software that combines real-time information (the status of first-responder units and facilities) with interactive content (information from citizens) and rich sources of data (satellite maps). Corporate communications monopolies will crumble as cities build their own emergency wireless networks using simple products from companies such as Proxim.

By 2016, we may see the trials of the previous decade as progress in disguise. The grassroots security effort will do more than just insulate our gas lines and high schools. It will also spur positive social change: so-called green systems will quickly shed their tree-hugger status and be seen as vital components of our economic and personal security. Even those civilian police auxiliaries could turn out to be a good thing in the long run: their proliferation—and the technology they'll adopt—will lead to major reductions in crime.

Some towns and cities will go even further. In an effort to bar the door against expanding criminal networks, certain communities will move to regulate, tax, and control everything from illegal immigration to illicit drugs, despite federal pressure to do otherwise. A newly vigilant and networked public will push for much greater levels of transparency in government and corporate operations, using the Internet to expose, publish, and patch potential security flaws. Over time, this new transparency, and the wider participation it entails, will lead to radical improvements in government and corporate efficiency.

On the national level, we'll see a withering of the security apparatus, and quite possibly a flowering in other areas. Energy independence and the obsolescence of conventional war with other countries will reduce tensions between the United States and the rest of the world. When the last of the oil is pumped out of the ground, corrupt states, which are now propped up by the energy income, will be forced to make the reforms they need to be accepted internationally, improving life for their people.

Perhaps the most important global shift will be the rise of grassroots action and cross-connected communities. Like the Internet, these new networks will develop slowly at first. After a period of exponential growth, however, they will quickly become all but ubiquitous and astonishingly powerful, perhaps as powerful as the networks arrayed against us. And so we will all become security consultants, taking an active role in deciding how it is bought, structured, and applied. That's a great responsibility and, with luck, an enormous opportunity.

NOTES

1. The Superempowered Competition

1. John Robb, "Security: Power to the People," *Fast Company,* March 2006.

2. Bill Joy, "Why the Future Doesn't Need Us," *Wired,* April 2000, www.wired.com/wired/archive/8.04/joy.html (accessed October 23, 2006).

3. "Military Fears over Playstation2," *BBC News,* April 17, 2000.

2. Disorder on the Doorstep

1. "Jordanian Firm Withdraws from Iraq," Associated Press, July 27, 2004.

2. Hadi Awad, "Suicide Attacker Explodes Car Bomb outside Police Station, Kills 68," Associated Press, July 28, 2004.

3. "Kremlin Hunts Down Chechen 'Bin Laden,'" *Sunday Herald* (Scotland), September 19, 2004, www.sundayherald.com (accessed October 23, 2006).

4. Thomas L. Friedman, *The World Is Flat: A Brief History of the Twenty-first Century* (New York: Farrar, Straus and Giroux, 2005). Friedman makes the case for a technologically enabled globalization that rips down borders.

5. Michael Scheuer, *Imperial Hubris: Why the West Is Losing the War on Terror* (Washington, DC: Brassey's, 2004).

6. Michael Ware, quoted in "Inside the Insurgency," *Frontline,* Fall 2005, www.pbs.org (accessed August 10, 2006).

7. "Baker Hughes Employee Killed in Nigeria As Unrest Continues," *Dow Jones,* May 10, 2006, www.wsj.com (accessed October 23, 2006).

8. Ware, quoted in "Inside the Insurgency."

9. "Bin Laden Lieutenant Admits to September 11 and Explains Al-Qa'ida's Combat Doctrine," Middle East Media and Research Institute, Special Dispatch 344, February 10, 2002, http://memri.org/bin/articles.cgi?Page=archives&Area=sd&ID=SP34402 (accessed October 23, 2006).

10. Ahmed Rashid, *Taliban: Militant Islam, Oil, and Fundamentalism in Central Asia* (New Haven, CT: Yale University Press, 2000).

11. William S. Lind et al., "The Changing Face of War: Into the Fourth Generation," *Marine Corps Gazette,* October 1989, www.d-n-i.net/ (accessed October 23, 2006).

12. Thomas X. Hammes, *The Sling and the Stone: On War in the 21st Century* (St. Paul, MN: Zenith Press, 2004).

13. Seymour Hersh, "Torture at Abu Ghraib," *New Yorker,* May 10, 2004, www.newyorker.com/fact/content/?040510fa_fact (accessed October 23, 2006).

14. "Full Transcript of Bin Ladin's Speech," *Al-Jazeera,* November 1, 2004, http://english.aljazeera.net/NR/exeres/79C6AF22-98FB-4A1C-B21F-2BC36E87F61F.htm (accessed October 23, 2006).

3. A New Strategic Weapon

1. Thomas P. M. Barnett, *The Pentagon's New Map: War and Peace in the 21st Century* (New York: G. P. Putnam's Sons, 2004).

2. George H. W. Bush, "Remarks at the United States Air Force Academy Commencement Ceremony in Colorado Springs, Colorado, 29 May 1991," *Weekly Compilation of Presidential Documents* 27, no. 22 (June 3, 1991): 685.

3. U.S. Department of Defense, *Final Report to Congress: Conduct of the Persian Gulf War,* April 1992, www.ndu.edu/library/epubs/cpgw.pdf (accessed October 23, 2006).

4. Sun Tzu, *The Art of War.* F. Andy Messing Jr., "Sustaining the Mission," *Washington Times,* November 17, 2004, www.washingtontimes.com (accessed October 23, 2006).

5. David A. Deptula, "Effects-Based Operations: Change in the Nature of Warfare," Aerospace Education Foundation, 2001, www.aef.org/pub/psbook.pdf (accessed October 23, 2006).

6. The United States Strategic Bombing Survey (European War) 1945, reprinted in the United States Strategic Bombing Survey (European War) (Pacific War) (Maxwell AFB, AL: Air University Press, 1987), p. 13.

7. Deptula, "Effects-Based Operations."

8. Charles Duelfer, *Comprehensive Report of the Special Advisor to the DCI and Iraq's WMD* (*Duelfer Report*) (Baghdad, Iraq: Iraq Survey Group, September 2004), p. 71, www.lib.umich.edu/govdocs/duelfer.html (accessed October 23, 2006).

9. This is an anecdotal story I heard from a friend who fought in the Gulf War.

10. Duelfer, *Duelfer Report,* pp. 71–72.

11. Vincent Brooks, "CENTCOM Operation Iraqi Freedom Briefing," U.S. Central Command, March 27, 2003.

12. James Glanz, "The Conflict in Iraq: Tactics; Insurgents Wage Precise Attacks on Baghdad Fuel," *New York Times,* February 21, 2005, http://travel2.nytimes.com/2005/02/21/international/middleeast/21sabotage.html?ex=1162443600&en=490040962edab068&ei=5070 (accessed October 23, 2006).

13. Jennifer Lovin, "Bush Gives New Reason for Iraq War," Associated Press, August 31, 2005.

14. Stephen Ulf, "Al-Zawahiri Encourages Targeting of Gulf Oil," *Terrorism Focus* 2, no. 23 (December 15, 2005), www.jamestown.org (accessed October 23, 2006).

15. Deborah Haynes, "Iraq Needs $20 Billion to End Chronic Electricity Crisis," *AFP Baghdad*, January 18, 2006, www.middle-east-online.com (accessed October 23, 2006).

16. Beth Potter, "Iraqi Voters under Pressure to Name Leaders," United Press International, March 30, 2005.

17. James Glanz, "Inching Along, One More Piece to Rebuild Iraq," *New York Times*, October 17, 2004, http://travel2.nytimes.com/2004/10/17/international/middleeast/17recon.html?ex=1162443600&en=b602c9c311d03e16&ei=5070 (accessed October 23, 2006).

18. "In the Line of Fire," *Atlantic Unbound*, June 15, 2004, www.theatlantic.com/ doc/200406u/int2004-06-15 (accessed October 23, 2006).

4. The Long Tail of Warfare Emerges

1. Philip Reeves, "U.S. Trying to Bridge Cultural, Military Divide in Iraq," *Morning Edition*, May 11, 2005.

2. P. Mitchell Prothero, "Coalition Losing War for Iraqi Arms," United Press International, September 29, 2003.

3. Alhaji Mujahid Dokubo Asari, "Oil Flowstations in Nigeria Shut Reopen: Official," Xinhua, September 26, 2005.

4. Tom Ashby, "Nigerian Delta Militants Evolve into Greater Threat," Reuters, January 20, 2006.

5. Stephen Ulf, "Thailand Crisis Deepening," *Terrorism Focus* 2, no. 21 (November 14, 2005).

6. Interview with Colombian paramilitary leader Carlos Castaño, Martha Elvira Soto F., and Orlando Restrepo, El Tiempo (centrist), Bogatá, Colombia, June 30, 2002, www.worldpress.org/Americas/648.cfm. Translated and posted to Worldpress.org July 15, 2002.

7. Russell Morse, "Mad Max in Borderland—Overnight with the Minutemen YO!" Youth Outlook Multimedia and New America Media, http://news.newamericamedia.org/news/view_article.html?article_id=329bbef27b902112e6d9882d04b74ddf, February 18, 2006.

8. Ibid.

9. http://www.blackwaterusa.com/ (no longer available).

5. Systems Disruption

1. Donald Rumsfeld, "War-on-Terror Memo," *USA Today*, October 16, 2003, www.usatoday.com/news/Washington/executive/rumsfeld-memo.htm (accessed October 23, 2006).

6. Open-Source Warfare

1. Scott Baldauf and Ashraf Christenson, "New Guns, New Drive for Taliban," *Christian Science Monitor,* September 26, 2005.

2. Eric S. Raymond, "The Cathedral and the Bazaar," *First Monday,* 1998, www.firstmonday.com/issues/issue3_3/raymond (accessed October 23, 2006).

3. Christopher Abad, "The Economy of Phishing," *First Monday,* June 14, 2005, www.firstmonday.com/issue10_9/abad/ (accessed October 23, 2006).

4. Sean J. A. Edwards, *"Swarming and the Future of Warfare,"* RAND, 2005, www.rand.org/pubs/rgs_dissertations/RGSD189/ (accessed October 23, 2006).

5. H. van Dyke Parunak, "Making Swarming Happen" (paper presented at the Conference on Swarming and C4ISR, Tysons Corner, VA, January 3, 2003, www.erim.org/ (accessed October 23, 2006).

6. Steven Johnson, *Emergence: The Connected Lives of Ants, Brains, Cities, and Software* (New York: Scribner, 2001), pp. 77–79.

7. Guerrilla Entrepreneurs

1. Dexter Filkins and Eric Schmitt, "14 US Marines Killed in Iraq When Vehicle Hits a Huge Bomb," *New York Times,* August 23, 2005.

2. Kathy Gannon, "U.N.: Taliban Virtually Wipes Out Opium Production in Afghanistan," Associated Press, February 16, 2001.

3. Juan Cole, "Max Boot Is Out of This World," Antiwar.com, September 11, 2003, www.antiwar.com /cole/?articleid=966 (accessed October 23, 2006).

4. Scott Atran, "Genesis of Suicide Terrorism," *Science* 299, no. 5612 (March 7, 2003).

5. Ralph Peters, "The New Warrior Class," *Parameters* (Summer 1994): 16–26, www.carlisle.army.mil/ (accessed October 23, 2006).

6. David E. Kaplan, "Paying for Terror," *U.S. News & World Report,* December 5, 2005.

7. John Robb, "The Open-Source War," *New York Times,* October 17, 2005.

8. David Kaplan, "Paying for Terror," *U.S. News & World Report,* December 5, 2005.

8. Rethinking Security

1. "Rumsfeld Ramble Wins UK 'Foot in Mouth' Award," Reuters, December 1, 2003.

2. Nassim Nicholas Taleb, "Learning to Expect the Unexpected," *New York Times,* April 8, 2004, http://query.nytimes.com/gst/fullpage .html?sec=travel&res=9C02E7DE1438F93BA35757C0A9629C8B63 (accessed October 31, 2006).

3. Department of the Army Field Manual 34–52, Intelligence Interrrogation, FM 34–52, ch. 1 (1987), available at www4.stmy.mil/ocpa/reports/ArmyIGDetaineeAbuse/FM34–52IntelInterrogation.pdf.

4. Bruce Schneier, *Beyond Fear: Thinking Sensibly about Security in an Uncertain World* (New York: Copernicus Books, 2003), p. 252.

5. Thomas P. M. Barnett, *Blueprint for Action: A Future Worth Creating* (New York: G. P. Putnam's Sons, 2005), pp. 51–52.

6. Barnett, *Blueprint for Action*, pp. 23–43.

7. Barnett, *Blueprint for Action*, pp. 315–327.

8. Thomas P. M. Barnett, *The Pentagon's New Map: War and Peace in the 21st Century* (New York: G. P. Putnam's Sons, 2004), pp. 258–267. Barnett provides a great discussion of the concept of system perturbations in this section.

9. Anne McGrath, "Individuals Key to Handling Emergencies," *U.S. News & World Report*, April 6, 2006.

10. Schneier, *Beyond Fear*, pp. 3–42. Schneier details the issues concerning the necessity for choices given limited means, subjectivity in trade-offs, and influence of power and agendas.

11. James Fallows, "Declaring Victory," *Atlantic Monthly*, September 2006.

12. Philip Bobbitt, *The Shield of Achilles: War, Peace, and the Course of History* (New York: Anchor Books, 2002), p. 669.

13. Bobbitt, *Shield of Achilles*, pp. 672–674.

14. Bobbitt, *Shield of Achilles*, p. 675.

15. Marco Iansiti and Roy Levien, *The Keystone Advantage: What the New Dynamics of Business Ecosystems Mean for Strategy, Innovation, and Sustainability* (Boston: Harvard Business School Press, 2004), pp. 43–57.

16. Ibid., pp. 112–122.

17. Ibid., p. 113.

18. Ibid., p. 115.

19. Ibid., pp. 82–105.

20. Ibid., pp. 93–95.

21. Calvert Jones and Sarai Mitnick, "Open Source Disaster Recovery," *First Monday*, April 20, 2006, www.firstmonday.org/issues/issue11_5/jones/ (accessed October 23, 2006).

22. If you want to learn more about the concept of brittle security, see Schneier, *Beyond Fear*, pp. 119–132.

9. A Brittle Security Breakdown

1. John Robb, "Security: Power to the People," *Fast Company*, March 2006.

FURTHER READING

Albert, Reka, Istvan Albert, and Gary L. Nakarado. "The Structural Vulnerability of the North American Power Grid." American Physical Society, February 26, 2004.

Arquilla, John, and David Ronfeldt, eds. *Networks and Netwars: The Future of Terror, Crime, and Militancy*. Santa Monica, CA: RAND, 2001.

Barabasi, Albert-Laszlo. *Linked: How Everything Is Connected to Everything Else and What It Means for Business, Science, and Everyday Life*. New York: Plume, 2003.

Barnett, Thomas P. M. *Blueprint for Action: A Future Worth Creating*. New York: G. P. Putnam's Sons, 2005.

———. *The Pentagon's New Map: War and Peace in the 21st Century*. New York: G. P. Putnam's Sons, 2004.

Bey, Hakim. *T.A.Z.: The Temporary Autonomous Zone, Ontological Anarchy, Poetic Terrorism*. Brooklyn, NY: Autonomedia, 1991.

Bobbitt, Philip. *The Shield of Achilles: War, Peace, and the Course of History*. New York: Anchor Books, 2002.

Brookings Institution. "The Iraq Index: Tracking Reconstruction and Security in Post-Saddam Iraq." Brookings Institution. www.brookings.edu/fp/saban/iraq/indexarchive/htm.

Bunker, Robert J., ed. *Networks, Terrorism, and Global Insurgency*. London: Routledge, 2005.

———, ed. *Non-state Threats and Future Wars*. Portland, OR: Frank Cass, 2003.

Chua, Amy. *World on Fire: How Exporting Free Market Democracy Breeds Ethnic Hatred and Global Instability*. New York: Doubleday, 2003.

Edwards, Sean J. A. *Swarming and the Future of Warfare*. Santa Monica, CA: RAND, 2005.

Friedman, Thomas L. *The World Is Flat: A Brief History of the Twenty-first Century*. New York: Farrar, Straus and Giroux, 2005.

Fukuyama, Francis. *The End of History and the Last Man*. New York: Free Press, 2006.

Hammes, Thomas X. *The Sling and the Stone: On War in the 21st Century*. St. Paul, MN: Zenith Press, 2004.

Huntington, Samuel P. *The Clash of Civilizations and the Remaking of the World Order*. New York: Simon and Schuster, 2003.

Iansiti, Marco, and Roy Levien. *The Keystone Advantage: What the New Dynamics of Business Ecosystems Mean for Strategy, Innovation, and Sustainability*. Boston: Harvard Business School Press, 2004.

Johnson, Steven. *Emergence: The Connected Lives of Ants, Brains, Cities, and Software.* New York: Scribner, 2001.

Liddell Hart, B. H. *Lawrence of Arabia.* New York: Da Capo Press, 1989.

———. *Strategy.* 2nd ed. New York: Meridian, 1991.

Lind, William S., et al. "The Changing Face of War: Into the Fourth Generation." *Marine Corps Gazette,* October 1989.

Luttwak, Edward N. *The Grand Strategy of the Roman Empire from the First Century A.D. to the Third.* Baltimore, MD: Johns Hopkins University Press, 1976.

Naim, Moisés. *Illicit: How Smugglers, Traffickers, and Copycats Are Hijacking the Global Economy.* New York: Doubleday, 2005.

Rashid, Ahmed. *Taliban: Militant Islam, Oil, and Fundamentalism in Central Asia.* New Haven, CT: Yale University Press, 2000.

Raymond, Eric S. "The Cathedral and the Bazaar." *First Monday,* 1998. www.firstmonday.com/issues/issue3_3/raymond.

Rheingold, Howard. *Smart Mobs: The Next Social Revolution.* Cambridge, MA: Basic Books, 2003.

Richards, Chester W. *Neither Shall the Sword: Conflict in the Years Ahead.* Washington, DC: World Security Institute's Center for Defense Information, 2005.

Robb, John. "The Open-Source War." *New York Times,* October 17, 2005.

———. "Security: Power to the People." *Fast Company,* March 2006.

Schneier, Bruce. *Beyond Fear: Thinking Sensibly about Security in an Uncertain World.* New York: Copernicus Books, 2003.

Singer, Peter W. *Corporate Warriors: The Rise of the Privatized Military Industry.* Ithaca, NY: Cornell University Press, 2003.

Taleb, Nassim. "Learning to Expect the Unexpected." *New York Times,* April 8, 2004.

Van Creveld, Martin. *The Rise and Decline of the State.* New York: Cambridge University Press, 1999.

———. *The Transformation of War.* New York: Free Press, 1991.

INDEX

Abad, Christopher, 119–120
Abu Ghraib torture, 29, 70, 157
Afghanistan
 al-Qaeda, 20–21, 138, 140, 143
 entrepreneurial warfare,
  142–144
 opium farming, 142–144, 150
Afghanistan war, 26, 70
Ahmidan, Jamal "El Chino,"
  150–151
airpower. *See also* warfare
 Iraq War (2003–), 41, 42–43
 Persian Gulf War (1990–1991),
  39–41
 Spanish civil war, 48
 strategy, 39
 technology, 38–39
 World War II, 37–38, 41
Al Ansar (al-Qaeda newsletter),
  20
Alaskan oil pipeline, 182
Albert, Istvan, 104
Albert, Reka, 104
Alexander the Great (king of
  Macedonia), 122
Al-Fallujah, Iraq siege, 58
Algerian war, counterinsurgency,
  111–112
Allegro Energy Group, 105–106
Allen, Chris, 140–141
Al-Muqrin, Abdul Aziz, 55
al-Qaeda
 Afghanistan, 20–21, 138, 140,
  143
 Bush, George W., 50
 funding of, 4–5, 150
 gang warfare, 93
 goals of, 17–18
 Iraq insurgency, 50–51
 open-source organization, 116

 organization of, 137–140
 small groups, 75
 warfare, 20–21, 30–32, 68
al-Qaeda in Iraq, 113, 118
Anderson, Chris, 71–72
Anderson Consulting, 97
Ansar al-Sunna, 118
Arafat, Yasser, 147
arms trade, globalization, 149
Aryan Brotherhood, 93
Ashby, Tom, 83
Assad, Hafez, 69
assassination tactics. *See*
  hostage/assassination tactics
Atlantic Unbound (Kaplan), 59
Atta, Mohammed, 139
Autodefensas Unidas de Colombia
  (AUC, United Self-Defense
  Forces of Colombia), 61, 86,
  88–89
avian flu, 153, 160, 162

Baath Party (Iraq)
 al-Qaeda, 18
 Iraq insurgency, 74, 78
Baloch tribesmen (Pakistan),
  83–84, 103–104
Ba'quba, Iraq, attacks in, 13–14,
  112
Barabaski, Albert-Laszlo, 101
Barnett, Thomas P. M., 158–160
Basayev, Shamil, 14
Bashir, Bakar, 148
bazaar analogy, open-source
  warfare, 117–119
Beslan, Russia massacre, 14
*Beyond Fear: Thinking Sensibly
  about Security in an
  Uncertain World* (Schneier),
  157–158

bin Laden, Osama, 17–18, 20–21, 30, 49, 112, 113, 139
blackout of August 2003 (U.S.), 96–97, 110
black swan events. *See also* security requirements
costs of, 109
security breakdown, 184–188
security requirements, 153–155
systems theory, 159–160
Blackwater (private military company), 89, 90, 185
blitzkrieg warfare, 22, 31, 95–96
blowback, paramilitary proxies, 61
Blueprint for Action: A Future Worth Creating (Barnett), 158–159
Bobbitt, Philip, 165–167
Bremer, Paul, 77
brittleness concept, 156–162. *See also* security requirements
breakdown in, 184–188
knee-jerk police states, 156–158
preemptive war and nation-building, 158–162
Buffett, Warren, 185
Bush, George H. W., 35, 36
Bush, George W.
al-Qaeda, 50
Foreign Intelligence Surveillance Act (FISA), 157
Iraq insurgency, 49
Iraq War (2003–), 34, 47
preemptive war and nation-building, 158–162
caliphate, Islam, 18
Casablanca, Morocco attack, 151
cascade concept, systems disruption, 100–104
Castano, Carlos, 86
Caucasian Front (Chechnya), 81
Caucasus, systems disruption, 94

cell phones, control of, 85–86
Center for Cultural Conservatism, 22
Central American Free Trade Agreement (CAFTA), 170
Central Intelligence Agency (CIA), 143, 155, 157
Chechnya war, 14, 45, 81
China, 18, 25, 56
Internet, 169
Iran, 70
paramilitaries, 86–87
petroleum, 129
security breakdown, 186–187
U.S. military, 7
Civil War (U.S.), 22, 70
Cloudmark company, 119–120
cold war, 24–26, 152
Cole, Juan, 144, 146
Colombia, paramilitary proxies, 60, 61
communications
stigmergy, open-source warfare, 123–125
technology, 75
computer-assisted bombs, 38
coordination, open-source warfare, 123–125
corporations. *See also* private military companies (PMCs); *specific corporations*
hostage/assassination tactics, 54–57
private military companies (PMCs), 90–91
corruption, paramilitary proxies, 60–61
cost-benefit ratio, systems disruption, 98–104
counterinsurgency. *See also* Iraq insurgency; Iraq War (2003–)
Algerian war, 111–112
errors in, 75–76

counterinsurgency *(continued)*
  fourth-generation warfare, 27
  open-source warfare, 118
  paramilitary proxies, 59–61
counterterrorism, assassination
    tactics, 139
Count Tilly (Johann Tserclaes),
    67
Creveld, Marin van, 28–30
criminal economy. *See also*
    narcotics trade
  al-Qaeda funding, 4–5
  future of, 187–188
  gang warfare, 91–93
  globalization, 5–6, 148–151
  Iraq insurgency, 74
  mafia, 142
  nonstate actors, 17
  open-source warfare, 119, 128
  paramilitary proxies, 60–61
  phishing networks, 119–122
Cuba, 169
Custer, George, 122

Daoud and Partners, 13
decentralized security, 164–182
  future of, 187–188
decentralized warfare, 74–75
decision making, warfare, 70–71
Defense News, 135
democracy, Iraq War (2003–), 34
demography
  guerrilla warfare, 145
  Iraq insurgency, 75–79
Denmark, 67
Deptula, David A., 39–40,
    106–107
Doha Round (World Trade
    Organization), 169–170
dominator ecosystem, 177–178
Douhet, Giulio, 37
Drug Enforcement Administration
    (DEA), 150
drug trade. *See* narcotics trade

Duelfer, Charles, 42
Duelfer Report, 44
Dunbar number, 140–141

ecosystems, security requirements,
    decentralization, 176–179
effects-based operations (EBO),
    Persian Gulf War
    (1990–1991), 39–40, 42
efficiency, security requirements,
    163
electrical power
  blackout of August 2003 (U.S.),
    96–97, 110
  Haditha, Iraq battle, 133
  Iraq, 15
  Iraq insurgency, 52–54
  Persian Gulf War (1990–1991),
    35–36
  platform approach, 174–175
  sustainability concept, 181–182
  systems disruption, cascade
    concept, 100
  vulnerability of, 104–105
El Salvador, paramilitary proxies,
    60
*Emergence: The Connected Lives
    of Ants, Brains, Cities, and
    Software* (Johnson), 126–127
emergent intelligence, open-source
    warfare, 125–127
*End of History and the Last Man,
    The* (Fukuyama), 159
entrepreneurial market-state, 166,
    167
entrepreneurial warfare, 133–151
environment, open-source warfare
    coordination, 124–125
European Union, managerial
    market-state, 166–167
extraordinary rendition, 157

failed states, nonstate actors, 17–19
Fallows, James, 165

Fedayeen Saddam, 44, 77
Federal Bureau of Investigation
(FBI), 91, 155
Federal Reserve Bank of New
York, 108–109
Ferdinand II (Holy Roman
Emperor), 67
feudalism, 20
Foreign Intelligence Surveillance
Act (FISA), 156, 157
foreign policy, security
requirements, 157
Foreign Policy (magazine), 5
fourth-generation warfare, 26–30
Chechnya, 45
Hussein, Saddam, 44–45
Iraq insurgency, 34
France, 67
Algerian war, 111–112
World War II, 23–24
Fuerzas Armadas Revolucionarias
de Colombia (Revolutionary
Armed Forces of Colombia),
29, 30–32, 89
Fukuyama, Francis, 159
Fuller, J. F. C., 31

Gambino family, 142
gang warfare, guerrilla warfare,
91–93
gasoline. *See* petroleum
Gazprom pipeline, 94
generic networks, 122
Genovese family, 142
Georgia (Caucasus), systems
disruption, 94
Germany
blitzkrieg warfare, 22, 31, 95–96
Spanish civil war, 48
World War II, 23–24, 95–96
Ghurka mercenaries, 12. *See also*
private military companies
(PMCs)
Glanz, James, 54–55

globalization
criminal economy, 5–6, 148–151
guerrilla warfare, 14–16
markets, 3
market-states and minimalism,
165–171
nation-state, 17
platform approach to security
requirements, 171–176
primitive motivations, 144–146
security breakdown, 186–187
security requirements, 153
technology, exponential
paradox in, 10–11
warfare, 25, 29–32, 70–71
global warming, 153
Grant, Greg, 135
Grasse, Pierre-Paul, 123–124
Green WiFi Project, 182
Guderian, Heinz, 23–24, 31, 40,
95–96
Guernica, Spain attack, 48–49
guerrilla warfare. *See also*
entrepreneurial warfare;
open-source warfare; systems
disruption; warfare
Chechnya, 45, 81
criminal economy, 148–151
entrepreneurial model, 133–151
fourth-generation warfare,
26–30
gang warfare, 91–93
globalization, 14–16
hostage/assassination tactics,
54–57
Hussein, Saddam, 44–45,
76–77
Iraq insurgency, 51–54
nation-state, 20–21, 26
Nigeria, 82–83
open-source warfare, 116–117,
119
organizational structure,
137–142

guerrilla warfare *(continued)*
  Pakistan, 83–84
  paramilitaries, 86–89
  petroleum, 127–129
  private military companies
    (PMCs), 89–91
  security forces, 57–59
  social systems, 147–148
  spread of, 80–86
  Thailand, 80, 84–86

Habsburg empire, 67
hacking concept, open-source
  warfare, 116–117
Haditha, Iraq battle, 133–134
Haditha, Iraq massacre, 29
Halliburton, 12, 55
Hama bombing, Syria, 69
Hamas
  fourth-generation warfare, 29
  primitive motivations, 146
  social systems, 147–148
Harrigan, James, 108–109
Hersh, Seymour, 29
Hezbollah
  fourth-generation warfare, 29
  Lebanon war (2006), 161–162
  primitive motivations, 146
  U.S. Marine Corps barracks
    bombing, 27
Ho Chi Minh, 27
Honduras, paramilitary proxies, 60
hostage/assassination tactics
  counterterrorism, 139
  Iraq insurgency, 54–57
human rights abuses, paramilitary
  proxies, 61
Hurricane Katrina, 90, 160,
  179–180
Hussein, Saddam, 33, 34, 42, 43,
  44–45, 51, 74, 76, 135
Hussein, Uday, 44, 77
Hyderabad, India, terrorist threat,
  5–6

Iansiti, Marco, 176–178
Illicit: How Smugglers, Traffickers,
  and Copycats Are Hijacking
  the Global Economy (Naim),
  5, 148–149
immigration
  criminal economy, 149
  future of, 188
  paramilitaries, 87–88
Imperial Hubris: Why the West Is
  Losing the War on Terrorism
  (Scheuer), 17–18
improvised explosive devices
  (IEDs)
  Chechnya, 81
  entrepreneurial warfare,
    135–137
  Haditha, Iraq battle, 133–134
  open-source warfare, 118,
    119
  Thailand, 85
inclusiveness, security
  requirements, 163
India, 18
  Iran, 70
  petroleum, 129
  terrorist threat, 5–6
industrial warfare, 22
infrastructure
  Chechnya, 81
  hostage/assassination tactics,
    55
  Iraq insurgency, 14, 80
  Iraq War (2003–), 5–6, 12–13,
    15, 41, 46–47
  Nigeria, 82–83
  Pakistan, 83–84
  Persian Gulf War (1990–1991),
    42
  systems disruption, 5–6
  as weapon, 45–47
Intel, 10
intellectual property, criminal
  economy, 150

interdependence
  systems disruption, cascade
    concept, 103–104
  warfare, 70–71
Internet. *See also* technology;
    telecommunications
  fragmentation, 8
  improvised explosive devices
    (IEDs), 136
  long-tail markets, 71–73
  market-states, 168–169
  nation-state, 17
  open-source concept, 115–116
  phishing networks, 119–122
  platform approach, 172–173
  sustainability concept, 182
  systems disruption, cascade
    concept, 100
  technological globalization,
    10–11
  warfare, 29–30, 71
interstate highway system,
    systems disruption, cascade
    concept, 103
investment, open-source warfare,
    119
Iran
  Iraq insurgency, 50
  isolation of, 169
  Lebanon war (2006), 26
  nuclear weapons, 25–26, 41–42
  petroleum, 70
  U.S. Marine Corps barracks
    bombing, 27
  U.S. military, 7
Iraq
  nuclear weapons, 25
  paramilitaries, 87
Iraqi Army, Iraq insurgency, 77–78
Iraq insurgency. *See also*
    counterinsurgency; Iraq War
    (2003–)
  effectiveness of, 13–14
  growth of, 34–35

hostage/assassination tactics,
    54–57
Hussein, Saddam, 44–45
  lessons of, 49–51, 161
  loyalties, 79–80
  open-source warfare, 113–114,
    123
  organization of, 4–5, 15–16,
    135
  paramilitary proxies, 59–61
  petroleum, 51–52
  population characteristics,
    75–79
  private military companies
    (PMCs), 90
  security forces, 57–59
  Shiite militias, 61–62
  small groups, 73–75
  systems disruption, 5–6, 12–13,
    15, 47, 51–54, 99, 103,
    106–108
  Zarqawi, Abu Musab al-,
    112–113
Iraq War (1990–1991). *See* Persian
    Gulf War (1990–1991)
Iraq War (2003–). *See also*
    counterinsurgency; Iraq
    insurgency
  Abu Ghraib torture, 29, 70,
    157
  airpower, 41
  Haditha battle, 133–134
  Haditha massacre, 29
  implications of, 4, 8, 19
  infrastructure, 5–6, 12–13, 15,
    46–47
  lessons of, 49–51, 161
  nation-state, 68
  private military companies
    (PMCs), 90
  U.S. invasion, 34–35
  U.S. military, 7
  Zarqawi, Abu Musab al-,
    112–113

Islam. *See also* Shia Islam; Sunni
   Islam
  caliphate, 18
  opium farming, 143
  Thailand, 84–86
Israel
  Islam, 18
  Lebanon war (2006), 26,
    161–162

Jamestown Foundation, 81, 85
Japan, mercantile market-state,
   166
Johnson, Paul, 55
Johnson, Steven, 126–127
Jones, Calvert, 179
Jordan, 13, 112
Joy, Bill, 6
just-in-time consumption, 180–181

Kadhi , Sabah, 47
Kaplan, David, 150–151
Kaplan, Robert, 59
Katrina, Hurricane, 90, 160,
   179–180
The Keystone Advantage (Iansiti
   and Levien), 176–178
knee-jerk police states, security
   requirements, 156–158
Korea, mercantile market-state, 166
Kosovo war, 26
Krebs, Valdis, 137–138, 157
Kurds, security forces, 58
Kuwait, Persian Gulf War
   (1990–1991), 25, 33, 40, 43

landlord ecosystem, 177
Lawrence, T. E., 106, 134–135
Lear Siegler Services, 56
Leavitt, Michael, 162
Lebanon
  paramilitaries, 87
  U.S. Marine Corps barracks
    bombing, 27

Lebanon war (2006), 26,
   161–162
Levien, Roy, 176–178
Liddell Hart, B. H., 31, 106
Lind, William, 22, 24, 27, 31
*Linked: How Everything Is
   Connected to Everything Else
   and What It Means for
   Business, Science, and
   Everyday Life* (Barabaski),
   101
Linux software, 115, 117
London, England attack, 75
long-tail markets, warfare, 71–73
loyalties, Iraq insurgency, 79–80
Lucchese family, 142
Ludendorff, Erich, 48

madrassas, 138–139
Madrid, Spain attack, 4–5, 85,
   150–151
mafia, 142
managerial market-state,
   166–167
maneuver warfare, U.S. military,
   22
Manwaring, Max, 91–92
Mao Tse-tung, 20, 27
Mara Salvatrucha (MS-13, gang),
   91–92, 93
marker-based coordination,
   stigmergy, 124
market economy
  globalization, 3
  systems disruption, 95–96
  warfare, 71–73
market-states, security
   requirements, 165–171
Martin, Philippe, 108–109
martyrdom, Iraq War (2003–), 68
mass warfare, 22
media
  stigmergy, open-source warfare,
    124

systems disruption, 100
warfare, 70
mercantile market-state, 166, 167
mercenaries. *See* private military
  companies (PMCs)
Mexico, 128
minimalism, security
  requirements, 165–171
Minutemen (U.S. paramilitary),
  87–88
Minutemen (U.S. Revolutionary
  War), 123
Mitchell, William, 37, 48
Mitnick, Sarai, 179
modernization, primitive
  motivations, 144–146
Mohammad, Gul, 113
money laundering, criminal
  economy, 150. *See also*
  criminal economy; narcotics
  trade
Moore, Gordon E., 10
Moore's law, 10
morality
  Iraq insurgency, 80
  telephone security, 156–157
  warfare, 70
Morse, Russell, 87–88
Movement for the Emancipation
  of the Niger Delta (Nigeria),
  18–19, 82–83, 99
MS-13 (Mara Salvatrucha, gang),
  91–92, 93
Muhajer, Abu Hamza al-, 113
Mujahideen Corps, 13
Mukhabarat (Iraqi secret police),
  77
multinational companies,
  hostage/assassination tactics,
  56. *See also* corporations;
  private military companies
  (PMCs)
Muslim Brotherhood, Hama
  bombing, 69

Muslims. *See* Islam
mutual assured destruction,
  nuclear warfare, 25
My Lai massacre, 29

Naím, Moisés, 4–5, 148–149
Najeeb, Qais, 75
Nakarado, Gary L., 104
Napoleonic Wars, 22
narcotics trade. *See also* criminal
  economy
  al-Qaeda funding, 4–5
  globalization, 148–150
  paramilitaries, 89
nationalism
  market-states, 168
  preemptive war, 161–162
  warfare, 23
nationality, hostage/assassination
  tactics, 56
National Security Agency (NSA),
  156–157
national-security systems,
  confidence in, 6. *See also*
  security requirements
nation-building, security
  requirements, 158–162
nation-state
  breakdown in security in,
    184–188
  control by, 16–17, 28
  entrepreneurial warfare,
    142–144
  failed states, 17–19
  guerrilla warfare, 26
  market-state, 165–171
  paramilitaries, 86–88
  police states, security in,
    156–158
  preemptive war and nation
    building, 158–162
  security, 156–164
  security limitations in,
    162–164

nation-state *(continued)*
   warfare, 7–8, 20–21, 22–24,
      67, 71
natural gas. *See* petroleum
NetJets, 185
networks, systems disruption,
      cascade concept, 100–104
New Orleans, Louisiana,
      Hurricane Katrina, 90, 160
New Yorker magazine, 29
New York Times (newspaper), 29,
      47, 54–55
Nicaragua, paramilitary proxies,
      60
niche markets
   ecosystems, 177
   long-tail markets, 72–73
Nigeria
   guerrilla warfare, 82–83
   petroleum, 18–19, 99, 128
nine
   black swan events, 155
   cost-benefit ratio, 99, 109
   globalization, 3
   implications of, 6–7, 8
   national-security systems, 6
   organizational elements,
      137–139
   warfare, 31
nonstate actors. *See also* small
      groups
   failed states, 17–19
   nation-state and, 17
   warfare, 20–21
North American Free Trade
      Agreement (NAFTA),
      169–170
Northern Alliance (Afghanistan),
      143
North Korea, nuclear weapons,
      25–26, 41–42
nuclear power facilities, 100
nuclear warfare, 24–26, 41–42,
      69

oil. *See* petroleum
Omar, Mohammed, 142–143
openness, platform approach, 174
open-source networks
   Internet, 115–116
   security decentralization,
      179–180
open-source warfare, 111–129.
      See also entrepreneurial
      warfare; guerrilla warfare;
      systems disruption; warfare
opium farming, 142–144, 150
outsourcing, open-source warfare,
      119

Pacific News Service, 87–88
Pakistan, 19, 80
   Baloch tribesmen, 83–84,
      103–104
   guerrilla warfare, 83–84
   paramilitaries, 87
Palestinians, terrorism, 28
pandemics, 153
paramilitaries
   guerrilla warfare, 86–89
   Iraq insurgency, 59–61
Peace of Westphalia, 68
peak oil, 153
*Pentagon's New Map: War and
      Peace in the 21st Century,
      The* (Barnett), 158–159
Persian Gulf War (1990–1991), 25
   airpower, 39–41, 42–43
   ground operations, 43–44
   infrastructure, 45–46
   Kuwait invasion, 33
   U.S. air campaign, 35–37
Peshmergas (Kurdish security
      forces), 58
Peters, Ralph, 145–146
petroleum
   Chechnya, 81
   disruptions in, 6, 12–13,
      127–129

guerrilla warfare, 127–129
Iraq, 15, 51
Iraq insurgency, 51–52, 74–75, 99
Iraq War (2003–), 34
Nigeria, 18–19, 82–83, 99
Pakistan, 84
peak oil, 153
Persian Gulf War (1990–1991), 33, 35
preemptive war, 161
security breakdown, 186
sustainability concept, 181–182
United States infrastructure vulnerability, 105–106
warfare, 70–71
phishing networks, open-source warfare and, 119–122
platform approach, security requirements, 171–176
PlayStation 2, 9–10
police states
breakdown in, 184–185
security requirements, 156–158
population characteristics
guerrilla warfare, 145
Iraq insurgency, 75–79
Potter, Beth, 54
preemptive war, security requirements, 158–162
primitive motivation, entrepreneurial warfare, 144–146
private military companies (PMCs)
future prospects, 185
guerrilla warfare, 89–91
productivity, ecosystems, 176

qualitative coordination, stigmergy, open-source warfare, 125

quantitative coordination, stigmergy, open-source warfare, 124–125

Rahimi, Karim, 143
Raymond, Eric S., 117
religion
Iraq War (2003–), 68
Thirty Years' War, 67
Republican Guard (Iraq), 77
return on investment. See cost-benefit ratio
Reuters, 83
Revolutionary Armed Forces of Colombia (Fuerzas Armadas Revolucionarias de Colombia), 29, 30–32, 89
Revolutionary War (U.S.), 123
Richthofen, Wolfram von, 49
risk, black swan events, 153–155
robustness, ecosystems, 177
Rumsfeld, Donald, 62, 98, 153
Russia, 56
Chechnya, 45, 81
paramilitaries, 87
systems disruption, 94

sabotage. See systems disruption
Sadr, Muqtada al-, 147
Samarra mosque attack, 61–62
Saudi Arabia, 17, 55, 56
madrassas, 139
Persian Gulf War (1990–1991), 33, 46
petroleum, 128
scale-free networks, systems disruption, cascade concept, 100–104
Scheuer, Michael, 17–18
Schneier, Bruce, 157–158
schwerpunkt, 95–96. See also blitzkrieg warfare; systems disruption

security requirements, 152–183.
See also black swan events;
brittleness concept
breakdown, in nation-state,
184–188
confidence in, 6
sematectonic coordination,
stigmergy, open-source
warfare, 124
sexually transmitted disease
(STD), 102
Shehhi, Marwan al-, 139
Shell Oil, 19, 82, 99
Sherman, William T., 70
Shia Islam. *See also* Islam; Sunni
Islam
Iraq insurgency, 74, 80
Iraq War (2003–), 68
Persian Gulf War (1990–1991),
43
Sunni Islam and, 62, 80
*Shield of Achilles: War, Peace,
and the Course of History,
The* (Bobbitt), 165–167
Shlash, Mushsin, 52
Singapore, mercantile market-
state, 166
Skype company, 172–173
small groups. *See also* nonstate
actors
guerrilla warfare, 20–21
Iraq insurgency, 73–75
Iraq War, 15–16
technology multipliers, 6–9, 11
warfare, 71
smart bombs (computer-assisted
bombs), 38
Smith, Adam, 163
social systems, entrepreneurial
warfare, 147–148
Society for Worldwide Interbank
Financial
Telecommunications, 156

Somalia war, 26
Southeast Asian tsunami, 179–180
South Korea, 56
Soviet Union, 152
Spanish civil war, 47–49
state actors. *See* nation-state
stealth technology, 38
stigmergy, open-source warfare,
123–125
Strategic Studies Institute, 91–92
Sudan, al-Qaeda, 50
suicide bombings, Iraq War
(2003–), 68
Sunni Islam. *See also* Islam; Shia
Islam
Iraq insurgency, 74, 77, 78, 80
Iraq War (2003–), 68
Shia Islam and, 62, 80
Sun Tzu, 37
sustainability concept, security
requirements,
decentralization, 180–182
swarming tactic, open-source
warfare, 122–123
Sweden, 67
Syria
Hama bombing, 69
Iraq insurgency, 50
Lebanon war (2006), 26
U.S. Marine Corps barracks
bombing, 27
sysadmin concept, 160
system destabilization, 161
systempunkt. *See* systems
disruption
systems disruption, 94–110. *See
also* guerrilla warfare; open-
source warfare; warfare
Chechnya, 81
costs of, 32, 96–98
global guerrilla warfare, 14–16
Iraq insurgency, 47, 51–54,
74–75, 103, 106–108

United Press International (UPI), 54
United Self-Defense Forces of
    Colombia (Autodefensas
    Unidas de Colombia, AUC),
    61, 86, 88–89
United States
  Civil War in, 22, 70
  electrical power vulnerability,
    104–105
  entrepreneurial market-state,
    166
  Lebanon war (2006),
    161–162
  limitations of, 162–164
  paramilitaries, 87–88
  petroleum infrastructure
    vulnerability, 105–106
  preemptive war and nation-
    building, 158–162
  security breakdown, 184–188
urbanization
  security breakdown, 187–188
  systems disruption, 108–110
U.S. air campaign, Persian
    Gulf War (1990–1991),
    35–37
U.S. Department of Defense
    (DOD)
  confidence in, 6
  ecosystems, 178–179
  private military companies
    (PMCs), 90
U.S. Department of Homeland
    Security, 157–158, 160–161,
    184
U.S. Marine Corps barracks
    bombing, Hezbollah, 27
U.S. military

Iraq insurgency, 14, 75–79
nine, 6–7
reform in, 22
third-generation warfare, 24
wars of choice, 70
U.S. News & World Report
    (magazine), 150–151

Vietnam war, 26, 27, 29

Wallenstein, Albrecht, 67
Ware, Michael, 18, 19
warfare. See also airpower;
    entrepreneurial warfare;
    guerrilla warfare
  al-Qaeda, 20–21, 30–32, 68
  evolution of, 21–26, 69
  fourth-generation, 26–30
  globalization, 14–16
  market economy, 71–73
  nation-state, 7–8, 67
  small groups, 73–75
  wars of choice, 69–71
Washington, George, 20
Westphalia, Peace of, 68
Wikipedia, 115–116
Wired magazine, 71
World Trade Organization
    (WTO), 169–170, 179
World War I, 22, 23, 43, 48,
    106–107, 134–135
World War II, 22, 23–24, 71
  airpower, 37–38, 41
  Spanish civil war, 48

Zarqawi, Abu Musab al-, 18, 49,
    61, 112–113
Zawahiri, Ayman al-, 49

Iraq War (2003–), 5–6, 12–13, 42, 45, 46
Nigeria, 82–83
Pakistan, 83–84
petroleum, 127–129
Thailand, 84–86

Taiwan, mercantile market-state, 166
Taleb, Nassim Nicholas, 155
Taliban
  Afghanistan war, 70
  al-Qaeda, 20–21
  entrepreneurial warfare, 142–144
Tallinn, Estonia, 172–173
technology. *See also* Internet; telecommunications
  airpower, 38–39
  communications, 75, 85–86
  exponential paradox in, 9–11
  Hyderabad, India, 5–6
  markets, 3
  multipliers of, 6–9
  nation-state, 17
  open-source concept, 115–116
  systems disruption, 95
  warfare, 23, 30–32
Tedder, Arthur, 37
telecommunications. *See also* Internet; technology
  Persian Gulf War (1990–1991), 36
  security, 156–157
  sustainability concept, 182
terrorism. *See also*
  counterterrorism; entrepreneurial warfare; guerrilla warfare; open-source warfare; security requirements; systems disruption; warfare
  criminal economy, 5, 148–151
  defense against, 3–4

fourth-generation warfare, 26–30
funding of, 4–5, 150–151
guerrilla warfare contrasted, 14–15
open-source organization, 116–117
social systems, 147–148
Syria, 69
warfare, 21
Terrorist Early Warning Group, 171
Tesla Motors, 182
Thailand, 80, 84–86
Thirty Years' War, 67–68, 69, 71
Tilly, Count of (Johann Tserclaes), 67
Time magazine, 18
Tokyo, Japan, 70
torture, 29, 70, 157
Torvald, Linus, 117
transparency, platform approach, 173
transportation, Persian Gulf War (1990–1991), 36
trench warfare, 23, 43
tribalism, Iraq insurgency, 74
Triple Canopy (private military company), 89, 90, 185
Tserclaes, Johann (Count of Tilly), 67
Turkey
  paramilitaries, 87
  World War I, 106–107, 134–135
two-way interaction, platform approach, 173

uncertainty, black swan events, 153–155
United Nations
  opium farming, 143
  petroleum, 70–71

United Press International (UPI), 54
United Self-Defense Forces of
    Colombia (Autodefensas
    Unidas de Colombia, AUC),
    61, 86, 88–89
United States
  Civil War in, 22, 70
  electrical power vulnerability,
    104–105
  entrepreneurial market-state,
    166
  Lebanon war (2006),
    161–162
  limitations of, 162–164
  paramilitaries, 87–88
  petroleum infrastructure
    vulnerability, 105–106
  preemptive war and nation-
    building, 158–162
  security breakdown, 184–188
urbanization
  security breakdown, 187–188
  systems disruption, 108–110
U.S. air campaign, Persian
    Gulf War (1990–1991),
    35–37
U.S. Department of Defense
    (DOD)
  confidence in, 6
  ecosystems, 178–179
  private military companies
    (PMCs), 90
U.S. Department of Homeland
    Security, 157–158, 160–161,
    184
U.S. Marine Corps barracks
    bombing, Hezbollah, 27
U.S. military

Iraq insurgency, 14, 75–79
  nine, 6–7
  reform in, 22
  third-generation warfare, 24
  wars of choice, 70
U.S. News & World Report
    (magazine), 150–151

Vietnam war, 26, 27, 29

Wallenstein, Albrecht, 67
Ware, Michael, 18, 19
warfare. See also airpower;
    entrepreneurial warfare;
    guerrilla warfare
  al-Qaeda, 20–21, 30–32, 68
  evolution of, 21–26, 69
  fourth-generation, 26–30
  globalization, 14–16
  market economy, 71–73
  nation-state, 7–8, 67
  small groups, 73–75
  wars of choice, 69–71
Washington, George, 20
Westphalia, Peace of, 68
Wikipedia, 115–116
Wired magazine, 71
World Trade Organization
    (WTO), 169–170, 179
World War I, 22, 23, 43, 48,
    106–107, 134–135
World War II, 22, 23–24, 71
  airpower, 37–38, 41
  Spanish civil war, 48

Zarqawi, Abu Musab al-, 18, 49,
    61, 112–113
Zawahiri, Ayman al-, 49

Iraq War (2003–), 5–6, 12–13, 42, 45, 46
Nigeria, 82–83
Pakistan, 83–84
petroleum, 127–129
Thailand, 84–86

Taiwan, mercantile market-state, 166
Taleb, Nassim Nicholas, 155
Taliban
  Afghanistan war, 70
  al-Qaeda, 20–21
  entrepreneurial warfare, 142–144
Tallinn, Estonia, 172–173
technology. *See also* Internet; telecommunications
  airpower, 38–39
  communications, 75, 85–86
  exponential paradox in, 9–11
  Hyderabad, India, 5–6
  markets, 3
  multipliers of, 6–9
  nation-state, 17
  open-source concept, 115–116
  systems disruption, 95
  warfare, 23, 30–32
Tedder, Arthur, 37
telecommunications. *See also* Internet; technology
  Persian Gulf War (1990–1991), 36
  security, 156–157
  sustainability concept, 182
terrorism. *See also* counterterrorism; entrepreneurial warfare; guerrilla warfare; open-source warfare; security requirements; systems disruption; warfare
  criminal economy, 5, 148–151
  defense against, 3–4

fourth-generation warfare, 26–30
  funding of, 4–5, 150–151
  guerrilla warfare contrasted, 14–15
  open-source organization, 116–117
  social systems, 147–148
  Syria, 69
  warfare, 21
Terrorist Early Warning Group, 171
Tesla Motors, 182
Thailand, 80, 84–86
Thirty Years' War, 67–68, 69, 71
Tilly, Count of (Johann Tserclaes), 67
Time magazine, 18
Tokyo, Japan, 70
torture, 29, 70, 157
Torvald, Linus, 117
transparency, platform approach, 173
transportation, Persian Gulf War (1990–1991), 36
trench warfare, 23, 43
tribalism, Iraq insurgency, 74
Triple Canopy (private military company), 89, 90, 185
Tserclaes, Johann (Count of Tilly), 67
Turkey
  paramilitaries, 87
  World War I, 106–107, 134–135
two-way interaction, platform approach, 173

uncertainty, black swan events, 153–155
United Nations
  opium farming, 143
  petroleum, 70–71